Making A Difference

Making A
Difference

WHILE YOU'RE
MAKING A LIVING

David Bertrand

with J. MARK BERTRAND

NEW PARADIGM PUBLISHING
HOUSTON, TEXAS
http://www.new-paradigm.com

Copyright ©1998 by David Bertrand
First Edition, 1998
Printed in the United States of America

ISBN 0-9666773-0-7
Library of Congress Catalog Card Number: 98-87460

For my partners

JANA MITCHAM &

TOM 'BIG AL' SCHREITER

for helping me make a difference.

CONTENTS

INTRODUCTION

In writing this book I have stood on the shoulders of giants. Whether or not I have seen farther than others is for you to discover as you explore these pages.

I began *Making A Difference* with a simple goal: to write the book I wish I'd been able to read when I first began my career in network marketing. Many of the ideas I have included in this book are not new, although I have tried to approach them in new ways. Marcel Proust wrote, "Our true voyage of discovery begins not in seeking new lands but in having new eyes." As I wrote this book, I did indeed develop 'new eyes.' As you read it, I encourage you to do the same.

Most books written about network marketing emphasize strategies for making more money, reaching more people, and moving more products. In *Making A Difference*, you will find a different approach.

When you start your own network marketing business, you leave behind the traditional business paradigm. When you leave that world behind, you must leave behind its thinking, too. Success in network marketing is often directly related to how well you make this transition. It's not always easy – you're learning a whole new approach to business, after all. This book serves as a companion to the process.

In 1984 I founded Nutrition For Life along with my partners Jana Mitcham and Tom Schreiter. At the time, one of our goals was to remove the physical 'failure factors' inherent in most other network marketing companies at the time. *Making A Difference* is another step in that direction, only this book tackles mental and psychological failure factors, the habits of thought which can sabotage a successful new venture.

How powerful are these mental factors? I have seen people spend years building a successful business, only to watch it self-destruct as a result of unseen failure factors. At the same time, I have seen people with no real expertise or experience succeed beyond all expectation simply by adopting new ways of thinking.

The thing that makes these new approaches successful is not that they are particularly unique or powerful – although in many cases they are. Their true effectiveness lies in the fact that they were developed within the network marketing community to address the real dynamics of this industry. Unlike methods borrowed from the traditional paradigm, these concepts are tailor-made for network marketing. They grew in popularity for the simple reason that they worked.

So many analogies have been used to explain network marketing that I wouldn't dream of throwing in another one at this point. Suffice it to say that your network marketing business is a lot like a low-risk franchise. It combines the freedom of being an entrepreneur with the security that comes from a well-tested concept. During the last two decades, network marketing has become a popular alternative for people who want to own their own business without putting themselves at the mercy of a high-risk start-up.

Most of these people have no prior experience with network marketing, so they aren't really prepared to make the transition. If you're one of them, or you're giving it some thought, this book will be an invaluable guide. If you've already started your own network marketing business, this book can provide advice, information, and insight gained during more than two decades in the industry.

No single book can answer all your questions or meet all your needs. But if you're interested in finding out how to replace hidden failure factors with winning strategies, this book is for you. If nothing else, it will live up to its name and make a difference in your life.

CHAPTER ONE

Making A Difference
or Making A Living:
A Modern Paradox

I WAS A HIGH SCHOOL TEACHER with a dream that was a lot bigger than my paycheck. My wife Judy helped put me through school, where I earned a Masters in Administration and Supervision in 1969. A few years later, we had two small boys to raise and a career to plan. Although I was starting out small, I had big plans. Standing in front of that class of high school students was just the beginning. One day, I would do something that would make all the people who had invested in me along the way proud.

One day I would make a difference.

For now, though, I was focused on something more modest – making a living. After all, I had mouths to feed and bills to pay. I had to keep my nose to the proverbial grindstone. Like most people, I made the common assumption that if I paid my dues, success would take care of itself.

Making a living occupied more of my time than I ever imagined it would. All those nights spent studying for tests, all those books to read and papers to write, all this education – I thought it would "pay off" a lot sooner. Instead, I found myself at the age of 34 still teaching high school. Today, it's a fact of life that teachers earn nowhere near in proportion to the contribution they make – a lesson I was about to learn the hard way.

I was fortunate in those days to have a mentor. His name was Dr. Bill Herring. He was the Choir Director at the school where I taught, and he had twenty years experience at the job. Dr. Herring was one of the most respected members of faculty – I was fortunate to have him as a friend. The thing that made Bill Herring such a special person was that he really made a difference at that school. He made an impact on both student and teacher alike. I wasn't the only teacher there who wanted to be another Dr. Bill Herring.

As small as it was, I was always grateful to get my paycheck. One afternoon I was leaving the school building, check in hand, on my way to the bank. I passed by Dr. Herring's office. He was just on his way out, with his own paycheck sticking out of his jacket pocket. We walked to the parking lot together.

I didn't know it, but that was destined to be the longest walk of my life. It was a walk that would take me from a gravel-paved parking lot in Southwest Louisiana to the helm of a multi-million dollar international corporation. And it started when Dr. Bill Herring tugged that paycheck out of his pocket and handed it to me.

"David," he said, "I've been teaching for twenty years. I'm at the top of my profession. One day, if you keep up the good work, you can do the same thing."

I didn't know what to say. I was flattered that Dr. Herring was saying this about me, but as I looked at that envelope in my hand – with his paycheck in it – I was a little confused. I tried to pass it back to him.

"I want you to take a look," he said.

We stopped on the gravel between my car and his. I weighed the envelope in my hand. The flap was open and I could just see the edge of the check. Looking inside that envelope was the last thing I wanted to do.

"Go ahead," Dr. Herring said. "I want you to know what it is you're working for. You have a family to support, a house to pay for. I know you're willing to work hard to get where I am today, and

I know that with twenty years under your belt, you can do it. Take a look at that check."

He spoke in a plain, matter-of-fact way, without any embarrassment. In all the conversations we'd had in the past, things had never taken this course before, but Dr. Herring had given me a lot of advice over the years, and it always turned out for the best. So I eased that check out of the envelope and looked down at it.

At first, I didn't look at the numbers. I said, "All right."

"Take a good look," Dr. Herring said.

And that's when I opened my eyes. At first, I thought there was a mistake. After all, Dr. Herring had a Ph.D. He was one of the senior members of the faculty and one of the most popular with the students. For a moment, I thought maybe by some freak accident his check and mine were switched. After twenty years, Dr. Herring was hardly making more than I was!

"I decided a long time ago that I wasn't in this for the money," Dr. Herring said, "and I know that you aren't either. But I thought you should know what to expect twenty years from now."

A MODERN PARADOX

Looking back, I don't know what made Dr. Herring decide to teach me that lesson. Whether he realized it or not, he was introducing me to one of the paradoxes of modern life. Today, most people have to make a choice between *making a difference* or *making a living*.

By default, we tend to choose making a living. After all, there are bills to pay, mouths to feed, obligations to keep. Making a living seems simple at first – it's just a matter of putting in your time, paying your dues. In the end, making a living becomes an all-consuming drive. We *have* more than any other generation before us, and we enjoy it much less. All we know is "making a living" – we don't know how to *live*.

The dilemma I faced as a young high school teacher was the same as the one faced by practically everyone. How could I think about making a difference in the world around me when my own family wasn't secure? How could I "give" when the people I loved were relying on me to "get." How could the impact I made on the life of a student at school make up for my inability to provide the best for the children at home? After Dr. Herring showed me his check, I sat in my parked car for a long time, trying to work it out.

I knew I wouldn't be the first teacher to leave for greener pastures. I'd seen friends of mine give up teaching to take higher paying jobs at the local chemical plant, in sales, or even working for themselves. In the past, I'd always felt that somehow they had made the wrong decision. But now, faced with the same choice to make that they must have faced, I couldn't be so sure.

I remember thinking, "You shouldn't have to choose. You ought to be able to make a difference *and* make a living."

Oddly enough, despite my education, I couldn't think of a single example where the two could co-exist. To make a difference often means to make a sacrifice. We're selfish by nature, so it's never easy to make a sacrifice – and it's not always a question of making a sacrifice by yourself. In my case, I was volunteering the whole family! And yet, making a sacrifice was exactly what it would take for me to make a difference.

Even very successful people have trouble balancing the need to make a living with the desire to make a difference. How many times have you heard of a millionaire bequeathing all his fortune to charity when he dies? You can't help but be struck by something like that – to spend your life amassing millions, and then to give it all away. That's impressive. Of course, in most cases, the millionaire is giving the money away only once he no longer needs it! He makes a difference, but only after the fact.

When you hear the phrase "making a difference," you probably think of some abstract act of charity, some "good deed." That's the definition most people use when they defend their choice to make a living rather than making a difference. They don't have the money to give to charity – they're just trying to get by themselves. They don't have time to worry about people they don't know who live on the other side of the world. It's amazing to me how far away we've managed to place those people who need that "difference," how impossible and unrealistic we've managed to make the simple act of helping out. Now, it's perfectly acceptable to think that "making a difference" is the concern of our church or our government – anyone's but ours.

In my business, I don't pull any punches. I try to be as vocal an advocate for making a difference as I can. I've been taken to task for this on a number of occasions, but there's one encounter I will never forget. It was a rainy day and I was trapped by the weather in a hotel lobby. My company, Nutrition For Life, was hosting its annual convention in the hotel, so I was able to pass the time with people I knew – distributors who had come from all over North America to attend the event. One of them, a very nice lady who had recently listened to a tape I'd made about our company's Core Values, started to explain that, as much as she'd like to leave a legacy and help people, she had to be more practical than that.

"I have to take care of my mother," she explained, "who can't get around good any more, and I'm putting my oldest daughter through college – which is a lot more expensive than when *I* was her age. I *believe* in that stuff – making a difference and everything – but honestly, I just don't have time! One of the reasons I'm here is I want to start making time to be able to do some of those things."

I was a little surprised. Here I was talking to a woman who was taking care of her invalid mother, putting her own daughter through college, and building a part-time business – and she was trying to *find time* to make a difference! She already *was* making a difference, and I told her so.

Making a difference means being there for the people who need you most. Sending your money around the world is no substitute for making a difference in the lives of the people around you every day. It's a virtue to dream big, but sometimes we let the size of our thoughts keep us from acting. As long as "making a difference" is something huge and abstract, something that takes place far away to people not at all like us, then there's nothing to keep us from just making a living. That's what most people do. And that's too bad.

Twenty years ago, I sat in my car and pondered what had just taken place. It seemed that Dr. Herring had just given me a choice – I could either make a difference or make a living. Contemplating that paycheck, I knew I had to do something – but choosing one path or the other seemed to mean too great a sacrifice. I wasn't willing to forgo making a difference and I wasn't about to stop making a living, either. I was trapped in the modern paradox.

I didn't realize it at that moment, but my life would never be the same. The journey that started when Dr. Herring and I walked across that parking lot would lead to some of the most exhilarating and most trying times in my life. I was taking a new direction, stepping out into territory that few people had crossed before.

My goal – my mission – was to resolve that paradox, to find a way to make a difference *and* make a living. This book is for those of you who, like me, are not willing to settle for one without the other.

MAKING A LIVING ISN'T ENOUGH

AT SOME POINT IN LIFE, we all experience that rare glimpse into the future when daydreams and wishful thinking clear to reveal a true picture of life twenty or thirty years from now. For most of us, it's a sobering revelation. We realize that, at the rate we're going, none of our dreams are going to come true. None of the expectations we had when we started out will be fulfilled. Unless some radical change takes place, all of our hopes for the future will come to nothing.

When this startling vision of the future came to me, I was standing in a high school parking lot. My mentor, Dr. Bill Herring, had just shown me the size of his paycheck – after more than twenty years, just a few dollars more than I was earning. I realized at that moment that, as the saying goes, if I continued to do what I'd always done, I'd continue to get what I'd always got. And it definitely wasn't enough.

The irony was, I was on the right track. I was advancing along my chosen career path. I liked my job. I enjoyed working with kids, seeing the difference I made in their lives. I knew there were professions that paid more, but nobody goes into education expecting to earn that kind of money. You choose a career in teaching because you want to help young people. You want to see them grow and develop. You want to put your mark on the next generation of leaders.

At the same time, I had a family to think of. I couldn't see myself supporting my growing family ten or fifteen years down the road with a paycheck like the one Dr. Herring had just showed me. If I couldn't do that as a teacher, then I would have to find another profession.

After all, I wouldn't be the first teacher to leave the classroom in search of a better career. And I wouldn't be the first to feel guilty about it.

I guess the next sentence in this story should read, "The very next day, I decided to start my own company." But, it doesn't. Like many people, I'd gotten a glimpse of what was in store, and deep down I knew that I had to do something. But, like most people, I put it off. I had experienced my wake-up call and gone right back to sleep.

HITTING THE SNOOZE BUTTON

MOST ALARM CLOCKS TODAY are equipped with a 'snooze' button. When the alarm sounds, you roll over and hit this button, and it gives you an extra ten minutes before the alarm goes off again. Whoever invented the snooze button hit on a remarkable feature of human nature: we have no trouble putting off what's important, as long as we can tell ourselves we'll do it eventually.

I remember a conversation I had years ago with a good friend of mine. I had just made the observation that the world is divided into two types of people – entrepreneurs and everyone else – and he made this comment: "David, everyone is an entrepreneur on the inside, only most people *keep* it inside." In other words, when most people hear the wake-up call, they hit the snooze button.

My story is the perfect example. I can't think of a more graphic revelation than having your mentor and role model – the person whose steps you're following in – show you his disappointing paycheck. If that doesn't galvanize you, if that doesn't drive you to action, nothing will. Well, it certainly gave me something to think about. Unfortunately, for a while, thinking about it was *all* I did.

I've never met a person who didn't, at one time or another, dream about getting out on their own. I've never met a person who wasn't dissatisfied in one way or another with their nine-to-five job. I've never met a person who wasn't convinced that their current career path tapped only a small part of their full potential. On the other hand, I've met only a handful of people who were doing something about it. Like me, they had come to realize what was at stake. They knew something had to be done. But they weren't ready to act.

GETTING READY

SOCIETY TODAY IS PACKED with people who are 'getting ready.' They've got big plans. They're going to make a big impact. They're going to impress everyone they know. No, they aren't quite ready to start. But, they're getting ready. How are they getting ready? Well, not in any particular, systematic way. Maybe they're just waiting until the timing is right. Maybe they're just waiting until their own life is under control. They can't really do anything with the way things are now, but they're *going* to do something . . . when they're "ready."

In the network marketing industry, we encounter this phenomenon all the time. Your friend admits that he isn't satisfied with his job. He knows he needs to make a change. He admits that the opportunity you've showed him is interesting – he's even impressed by the results you've seen so far. But, you know, he's just not ready. He still has things to work out in life, he's still got to think some things through. He's going to take action – that's for certain, he says – but right now, he's still getting ready.

Looking back, I consider every day that passed between my conversation with Dr. Herring and the moment I finally took action to be wasted. All the time I spent preparing myself, thinking things through, getting myself ready, all of it was thrown away. Nothing I did during that period had any positive impact on my future. I didn't gain anything by delaying. Now, in retrospect, I can say that, no matter what I was telling myself, I wasn't "getting ready." The fact is, like most people, I had awakened to an unpleasant reality and, instead of taking on the challenge, I hit the snooze button and went back to sleep. Fortunately for my family and me, I didn't stay that way. But I was an exception. Most people who hit that button will hit it again, and again. By the time they get up, it will be too late, twenty or thirty years too late. You spend twenty or thirty years thinking of what you could do, and suddenly one day you're thinking of what you should have done.

I'm here to tell you it doesn't have to be that way. Here are two rules you should make a part of your thinking:

1. NEVER WAIT UNTIL YOU'RE READY

Motivational speaker Les Brown says it best: "Make your move before you're ready." Why? Because you will *never* be ready if you wait. The whole idea of 'getting ready' is a lie your mind tells you to justify inaction. Think about it: conditions will never be perfect, or even ideal. You will always face challenges. If you wait for a break in the clouds, you'll always find an excuse not to start.

Don't wait until your life is in order. Your life is probably in as good an order as it will ever be. We all dream of living tranquil lives, but the fact is, if you wait for tranquility before you take action, you will be waiting forever. (And if you ever achieve it, taking action will only disrupt the harmony!) When it comes to changing your life for the better, it's hard to make excuses. Instead of waiting for circumstances to change, take action. One of the thrilling things about the life of an achiever is the way that 'circumstances' seem to resolve themselves in the face of determined action.

Don't wait until you're better prepared. I have the deepest sympathy with people who want to improve their weaknesses before they start out on any venture. I've always been very conscious of my weaknesses. By nature, I'm a 'relater.' I would much rather share stories than get down to business. I would much rather preserve relationships than take decisive action. That's the way I am, and rather than waiting until that changes, I've learned to accept my weaknesses and emphasize my strengths. Peter Drucker dedicated a chapter in *Managing For Results* on the topic of 'building on strengths,' a common theme of his. He points out that the formula for success in putting together teams is not to eliminate weakness but to emphasize strength. We all have weaknesses, and if we wait until we overcome them we'll wait forever. Instead, learn to develop your strengths. The best way to do this, of course, is to take action.

2. NEVER WAIT UNTIL THE TIMING IS RIGHT

Inaction is the greatest enemy in any endeavor, and its accomplice is timing. We often use timing as an incentive – "Get in now while the timing's right." For the achiever, the timing is always right, because the achiever tells time according to his or her own clock. For everyone else, the timing is *never* right, or so it seems.

The truth is, the advantages derived from good timing are marginal. Yes, there are benefits to being in on the 'ground floor,' but they are *conditional* benefits. For my part, I have to confess that I've never worried about being on the 'ground floor' of anything. And yet, I've always been successful. Why? Because a long time ago, I learned to make my own timing.

On the other hand, I know people my age who've put the last twenty years into someone else's company, and as they get closer and closer to retirement, they're suddenly 'open' to opportunity. These are the same people who were waiting for the timing to be right when I tried to get them involved in network marketing in the 1970s. Here's a tip: everyone's waiting for the timing to be right – you're better off starting *before* the timing's right so you can get a jump on them!

CIRCLES OF INFLUENCE

IN 1984, WHEN I HELPED FOUND Nutrition For Life, the company's mission statement came directly from the dream I shared with my partners: "Nutrition For Life is committed to making a difference in people's lives by offering a realistic opportunity to achieve better health and financial independence." Over the years, that statement has been shortened in people's minds to "making a difference in people's lives" or just "making a difference." Nutrition For Life has been associated with those words in the same way Ford says "Quality is Job #1" and Nike says "Just Do It".

But 'making a difference' can mean a lot of different things. In a sense, we all make a difference in people's lives. Everything we do, no matter how small, that has an impact on the world around us makes a difference. No one needs a book to show him or her how to do this. It comes naturally. Sometimes our actions make a positive impact on people around us, sometimes they have a negative effect. Either way, for better or worse, they make a difference.

Each of us has a circle of influence that consists of the people whose lives we touch on a day in, day out basis. The size of this circle varies from person to person, but it includes your family, your friends and neighbors, your co-workers, and people you meet from time to time. Some people in your circle – your children, for example – are highly influenced by your decisions. Others, like your neighbors and acquaintances, are only partially influenced by the things you say and do. We often underestimate the influence we have over others. The influence of your example – even without additional influences – can have a major impact on the people in your circle.

In network marketing, you may come to think of your circle of influence as your "warm market." These are people you know and feel comfortable talking to about your business opportunity. As your business grows, your circle of influence will expand. Many of us have a hard time defining our circle of influence. I've always thought that the best way to identify your own circle of influence is to try and pick out someone else's.

After all, you're a part of someone else's circle of influence. In fact, you're a part of many circles. Just think of all the people whose actions and example influence you! If you think of a person who influences you, and then think of other people influenced by that same person, you'll begin to appreciate just how large these circles can be. Now, start thinking of your own circle – family, friends, people at work or school, people who may not even know you but know *of* you. These are the people in whose lives you can most easily make a difference.

By definition, we all make a difference in our own circle of influence. A few of us manage to make a difference outside our circles – with people we've never met or, in some cases, with generations not yet born. When I think of some of the people who've made a difference in my life, it's amazing how many of them died before I was ever born – but lived on to influence me through their books or their children or the legacy they left behind.

Making a difference means having a positive impact on another person. It means helping people – physically, emotionally, spiritually. It also means experiencing a change in yourself. If you take the things you learn here and apply them in your life, you won't remain the same. You will grow and develop, just as I grew and developed when I first began this journey. In writing this book, I am inviting you to join me in an unusual and exciting quest. I invite you to make a difference not only in other people's lives but in your own life, too.

THE PRACTICAL VISIONARY

THE FIRST TRANSFORMATION that's necessary to make the leap from the traditional business paradigm to network marketing is to become a *practical visionary*. The world where 'making a living' reigns is imminently practical, and the world of 'making a difference' is, above all, visionary. To manage the transition to a networking paradigm, you've got to combine the two and become a practical visionary.

When I talk about 'making a difference,' I expect a certain amount of skepticism on the part of the person I'm talking to. As a rule, we all try to be down to earth. We try to be realistic, especially when we're evaluating what someone else has to say. When you hear someone talk about "making a difference," a red flag goes up. Is this for real? After all, the reason most people's dreams don't come true in life is that, well, dreams *don't* come true, right? That's not what real life is about. In the real world, when you want to get ahead, you expose yourself to a lot of risk. Nine times out of ten, you lose, and all that risk turns into catastrophe. Now, here comes someone saying you should get out on your own, run the risk, be your own boss, make your dreams come true, make a difference. Isn't that a little unrealistic? Isn't that wishful thinking? Isn't it a little naïve?

I like to think that my philosophy of life is a little unique, because it brings together two things that most people believe are not alike at all: making a difference and making a living. In other words, I combine practicality and optimism, the real and the ideal. Without vision, even the most capable people never rise above mediocrity. Without practicality, even the greatest visionaries never leave an indelible mark on the world. To grasp my philosophy of achievement you must stop thinking of making a difference and making a living as opposites. In fact, they are two sides of the same coin.

An interesting trend in the publishing world recently has been the appropriation of military treatises as business textbooks. You may have heard of *The Art of War* and *The Book of Five Rings*, not because of what they say about military strategy but because they've been borrowed so effectively by business thinkers. Recently, Currency Doubleday published the Marine Corps manual *Warfighting* as a business title! I have to confess that I haven't delved very deep into this trend. Despite a brief tour in the Navy as a young man, I've never been too adept at military thinking, but I do have a great admiration for the model of achievement the military has given us.

Think about it: what other organization could convince thousands of young men to successfully complete all kinds of complex, dangerous tasks – and to get them not only to do it but to *want* to do it! The modern military is a feat of organization, and I've remembered enough of my own Navy training to make an application.

Your business, believe it or not, is like an army. It's your tool for achieving certain objectives. Now, like most armies, its effectiveness depends largely on two factors: the quality of its leadership and the existence of its supply lines. In other words, it relies on both the visionary and the practical aspects of achievement.

Without lines of supply and good logistics, your business will starve to death before it ever fights a battle. That's what's wrong with a business led by dreamers: They do fine in the parade, but when it comes to actually marching, their blisters get the better of them. They start out with great expectations and end up nowhere. They have the motivation and the vision, but they don't have the practical skills to keep the business going.

On the other hand, a well-supplied business is useless without inspired leadership. That's the problem with a business run by 'realists.' The supply lines are there, but there's no direction, no impetus for successful expansion. A business in the hands of practical caretakers may maintain itself, but to no purpose – and it certainly won't grow. No greater catalyst for action exists than shared vision. Without vision, you can't sustain your action, you can't renew your strength. Without a vision, the people, no matter how great they are, perish.

But when you take that practical concern for taking care of details and combine it with visionary leadership, you get an awe-inspiring organization, the kind that can win real victories.

To make a difference *and* make a living, you need the qualities of a good general. You need practicality, good sense, tenacity, audacity, the courage to look fear in the face, the wisdom to choose which fights to make, and the talent of spotting quality people and elevating them as your lieutenants.

To make a difference *and* make a living, you must transform yourself, simply put, into a practical visionary.

TAKING ACTION

THE MOMENT I SAW Dr. Bill Herring's paycheck, I knew I had to make a change. Yes, I hit the snooze button a few times. Yes, I used all the excuses – "I'm waiting until I'm ready," "I'm waiting until the timing's right." But in the end, I made a decision that was to shape the course of my life.

I didn't have the money to start my own business, and I wasn't willing to take the risks. Part-time work in addition to teaching was an option, but not a good one. How could I support my family if I never saw them? I gave a lot of thought to getting a new job, maybe in sales. I'd been in sales off and on in the past, when I was in school, and I'd always been good at it. In the end, that didn't feel right, either.

I'd been toying with these options for a while when someone mentioned network marketing. I knew people who'd tried network marketing before – tried and failed – so at first I wasn't too keen. The thing that finally won me over was the concept itself and how well it fit with my situation. I could start a business of my own part-time, right now. I wouldn't have to raise investment capital or borrow any money. If I did well, I could expand by business by putting more time into it. If I didn't do well, I would only be out a fraction of what I would risk with any other option.

Looking back, I don't know how I managed to be as successful as I was. I didn't know anything about the industry. I made all kinds of mistakes. Maybe my enthusiasm won over my inexperience. Maybe it was meant to be. All I know is, the more I came to understand network marketing, the more I became convinced that there was something unique at work. I found myself sharing the plan with other people more and more, not out of a sense of obligation but from a sense of excitement. I have never been so enthralled by any concept in my life as I was by this. It was a revelation.

I found myself looking at other people and wondering, "Do they even *know* what's happening? Do they even *realize* what this is?" At the time, if you'd asked me what it was, I would have had a hard time putting it into words. I felt like I'd discovered a gold mine and I wanted everyone to know about it. Later, the experts and trend analyzers would come out with their predictions: "Multi-level marketing – the business of the 80s," "Network marketing – the wave of the 90s," and so on. By then, I had already gone from a network marketing distributor to founding a network marketing company – but that's a story I'll save for another chapter.

CHAPTER TWO
The Value of Values

IF YOU WANT TO BUILD a successful network marketing business, the one skill you should seek before all others is the ability to build relationships. The hierarchy of power that structures organizations in the traditional business paradigm does not exist here. No one works *for* anyone else. In a sense, network marketing is 'cooperative' marketing – we work together from self-interest. For a system like this to be effective, it must be founded on solid win-win relationships.

Judging by what we hear in advertisements, every business out there – from pest control to used car sales – is a 'people-helping-people' enterprise. In network marketing, this slogan is transformed into literal truth. Your own interests and those of your colleagues overlap in a way that, by helping them, you help yourself, and vice versa. Unlike the traditional paradigm, where people tend to be in competition, here you benefit from the success of others and they benefit when you advance. In an equation like this, we all end up winners.

When I realized this for the first time, the value of the network marketing concept really hit home. It was a business opportunity, but it was also more than that: it was an alternative to the corporate slash-and-burn style of business with which so many people were becoming disillusioned. In network marketing, your success didn't threaten someone else's livelihood – in fact, it strengthened it. To my mind, that was a revolutionary concept.

I expected a kind of business utopia when I started my first network marketing business. I was sponsored by my brother, and his enthusiasm soon rubbed off on me. The more I learned, the more I began to see myself as part of a larger group of like-minded entrepreneurs. I helped others with the confidence that, when I needed it, they would be there for me, too.

One thing I picked up on right away, though, was that some of the people involved in network marketing had not truly bought into the concept. Yes, they had started businesses, and some of them had begun to show the plan to others, but their outlook on life and perspective on business was unchanged. I encountered them at meetings and even ran into them in my own upline. The only word I can use to describe their attitudes is 'skeptical.' It was as if they were going through the motions without really believing it would work. I was puzzled, to say the least.

I didn't realize it at the time, but I was observing first hand a phenomenon that continues to this day – people bringing the old way of thinking to the new paradigm. Before long, I figured out how to diagnose this problem and to give it a name: *lack of belief.* Of course, it went even deeper than that. People lack belief because they lack understanding. How can they believe something will work if they don't understand it? On the other hand, I couldn't really claim to understand this new business – but I definitely had belief. What was different about my case? How was I able to develop a strong belief level when other people who seemed just as perceptive and able, if not more so, didn't manage to? What did I have that these people didn't have?

Two factors immediately came to mind: First, as a teacher, I had always understood the relationship between thoughts and action. I accepted that, taking part in a new kind of business, I would have to develop new ways of thinking to support my actions. Second, and perhaps most important, the person who introduced me to the business opportunity took the time to build a good relationship with me. I trusted him, and that trust helped me make the transition. Taken together, these two factors made it easy for me to develop a strong belief level where others found it more difficult. They were clinging to ineffective ideas imported from the traditional business paradigm, and they didn't have strong relationships with others involved in the new opportunity. Under the circumstances, their skepticism and subsequent lack of success was a foregone conclusion.

In modern society, we tend to underestimate the value of relationships. We feel more comfortable when we separate business from pleasure, even if it means extracting pleasure from most of our waking hours. We don't like the idea of personal relationships interfering with business decisions. We take exception to any form of advancement that is influenced by friendship or family ties. In the same way that we have tried to banish religious belief from the public square, we tend to place personal considerations on the margins of business, as if what we believe and feel had nothing to do with making good decisions.

At the same time, we know instinctively that we'd rather rely on people we trust. Given the choice, most of us would prefer to help a friend rather than a stranger. We would like to use what power and influence we have to assist our allies, and we'd like them to do the same for us. What this means is, we understand the importance of relationships, but we don't like to talk about them – especially not in a business context.

I have to confess that I've always mistrusted this two-sided approach to relationships. A few years ago, I took one of those personality tests that divide us all into categories – in this case directors, relaters, socializers, and thinkers. As the CEO of an international corporation, I was fully expecting to be ranked among the directors. Much to my surprise, however, I turned out to have a 'relater' personality – in other words, I was predisposed to see the world in terms of relationships. When I considered the fact that I was the CEO of an international *network marketing* company, it all made sense!

As an educator, I also knew that the students who learned the most in my classes were the ones I was able to build rapport with. I found that the more the students liked me, the more they listened to what I had to say. They even performed better because they didn't want to let me down. The same thing was true in athletics. If I could get my players to respect me and trust me, there wasn't anything they wouldn't do. Even when they thought they had nothing left to give, they'd go out there and work miracles if I told them they could do it. As long as I had strong relationships with them, they trusted me to lead them.

To succeed in network marketing, I transferred that understanding to my business. I used all the motivational skills I'd learned as a coach to keep people focused. I built rapport and used my relationships to transfer information and training. I knew that my belief level would rub off on other people if they were exposed to it through a strong relationship. There I was, a newcomer myself, acting as a mentor to everyone I met. It was an exhilarating experience to say the least. Even though I was guided by instinct and didn't really know what I was doing, my entire group began to benefit from the enthusiasm I brought to the table. People who'd been involved longer than me started meeting each other *through* me and building relationships of their own.

WHEN TO TALK ABOUT RELATIONSHIPS

RELATIONSHIPS ARE ONE OF THOSE THINGS that are easier to build if you don't talk about them. There are thousands of ways to build a relationship, and I think one of the least effective is to begin by saying, "I'd like to build a strong relationship with you." Relationships can't be forced, and people are turned off when they see you are consciously 'relating' to them. This is one of those areas where actions speak louder than words.

Another common pitfall is to *talk* about relationships without really *building* them. When you think in terms of romantic relationships, this is obvious. You can't just *say* you love someone – you have to *show* it. It takes attention and consideration and time. Think of how people in love agonize over whether or not it's time to tell each other about their feelings. Usually they're still worrying once it's become obvious to everyone else that they're in love. That's a characteristic of all relationships: you can only really talk about them once they're obvious to the world around you. Relationships in business, like all relationships, are built not with dialogue, but with deeds.

Today, there are hundreds of books on the market to teach us how to build loving relationships – how to love our spouses, how to love our children, how to love our parents – the list is endless. I haven't come across many that talk about how to love our colleagues and build strong working relationships with them. It's not surprising. Most business books are aimed at the traditional paradigm, where loving your colleagues and helping them advance is a good way to stay in the mailroom. Building business relationships is a skill that truly comes into its own in the hands of a network marketer.

You will need to build two very different kinds of relationships. First, because you will be introducing new people to the opportunity, you will need to be skilled at developing relationships with people who are potential colleagues. Then, because you will need to work well with people who have already embraced the opportunity, you will need to be skilled at building relationships with your fellow distributors. Of course, relationships of the first type can often develop into relationships of the second type.

The first relationship, the one you have with a prospective distributor – or even a new distributor just starting out – centers on the all-important theme of *trust*. After all, when you enter the world of network marketing, you encounter a whole new way of doing things. It's a fairly dramatic change. In the last chapter, we considered some of the challenges people face when it comes to making a change. To make it effectively, you need someone to guide you, someone you can rely on – someone you trust. How important is trust? I've heard it said that trust, or even relationships in general, are not essential to this process, because when people make a change, they do it for themselves, not for someone else. "It doesn't matter if they trust you, as long as they trust themselves." Well, they have a point, but they overlook the fact that many people take action *before* their belief level is high, before they trust themselves fully – and having someone you trust lead the way is an asset.

In the same way that prospective or new distributors need to know they can trust you, your colleagues in the business need to know that you are *committed*. In other words, they need to know that you share the vision. Over time, your colleagues will draw strength from your commitment, and you'll grow stronger because of them. Your relationships with people in your upline and downline act as conduits for belief. I learned this early on in my career, as I began to meet people who had been in the business longer than me. Just being around them got me excited. I sometimes drove hours to be at meetings, and I spent the whole way back thinking about how exciting it was to meet those leaders and get to talk to them. Later on, when I became one of them, they told me how seeing me drive all that way to the meeting and getting to talk to me got *them* fired up. The whole time I was feeding off their experience they were soaking up my enthusiasm! Through relationships, we sustained each other.

How were these relationships built? I demonstrated my commitment by driving from Louisiana to Mississippi on weekends to help a group there show the plan. Others showed their commitment to me by helping my personally sponsored distributors who lived too far from me build their own businesses. In other words, we gave proof of our commitment through action, and soon we came to rely on each other for support. These were very different business relationships from any I had experienced before. They were reciprocal, for a start. We were working together, but working for ourselves at the same time. Sometimes people I'd never met before or only knew as a voice on the telephone were helping my business grow. I did the same for them in return. It was truly unique.

The relationship I had with prospective and new distributors was unique as well. In a sense, I acted as a mentor. Keep in mind, however, that you don't *choose* to be a mentor – mentors are chosen by their students. If I wanted to enjoy the trust of my prospects and new distributors, I had to make myself an attractive mentor.

I've already introduced you to one of my mentors, Dr. Bill Herring. The thing that made Dr. Herring attractive to me as a mentor was that he took the time to understand my point of view. Now, he was far advanced along the road I was traveling, and he knew a lot more than I did. He could have shared that knowledge in any way he chose, and the method he decided on was sympathetic companionship. In other words, he shared my experiences, took the trouble to see things my way, and then added his own knowledge to the mix.

A mentor is much more than a teacher. You can learn from a teacher, but you can truly *relate* to a mentor. A mentor is a person in whose steps you want to follow. Most mentors act as friends to their students. They ignore the gap of age and experience that separates them and take an active interest in what their companion is doing. In fact, mentors often learn from you at the same time they teach. It's a reciprocal relationship.

I've found that when you make yourself available as a mentor, you attract those who are willing to listen. By sharing their experiences you create a bond of trust. That bond serves as the basis for the relationship, and that relationship often grows into a comfortable friendship. Although we often start out in awe of our mentors, we soon learn to accept them as friends and equals. As the relationship matures, we become colleagues – we learn to rely on each other's commitment for strength.

In a few pages, I've tried to sketch a picture of what is really a very complex and profound process. Of course, there's no way I can capture all its nuances, but I hope I've convinced you just how important relationships are to your success in network marketing. In fact, I would go a step further and say that knowing how to build relationships will be an advantage in anything you do. It's a skill that is well worth the time it takes to master.

THE FOUNDATION OF ALL RELATIONSHIPS

RELATIONSHIPS ARE NOT STATIC. They change and develop over time as they weather new experiences. Relationships must be maintained, or they will deteriorate. Fortunately, a good relationship, even when it falls into disrepair, is usually easy to re-establish.

Two of the most important business relationships in my life are the relationships I share with my partners Jana Mitcham and Tom Schreiter. Over the years, we've grown closer by facing adversity and abundance together. We've learned to rely on each other's judgement and ability. Together, we've accomplished much more than any of us ever expected. Our relationships have stayed strong because they are based on an indestructible foundation.

Some people understand this foundation intuitively, while others have to learn it. You will have to determine which group you belong to.

The foundation of strong relationships is a set of principles or values that transcend circumstance. If you're a parent, you know this already. Your love for your child is not contingent on the child's performance. You don't measure out your love in accordance with what each child 'deserves.' The relationship is separate from the circumstances, because it is founded on the principle of unconditional love.

I've always been loyal to my friends. In fact, I've stayed true to friends even at the risk of criticism. When people ask, "Why are you sticking with this person?" I can honestly answer, "Because I'm sticking with my principles." When a relationship is built on firm principles, staying true to it is a question of staying true to yourself.

Remember, you don't build relationships with people because they're perfect. If that was your criteria, you couldn't even have a relationship with yourself! Instead, you build relationships to help people, and to insure that you'll have help when you need it. One thing I've learned over the years is that the relationships you stick with through adversity are the ones that produce the most benefit in the long run.

Now up to this point, most people would agree with me – as long as we're confining ourselves to *personal* relationships. But surely we aren't expected to stick with a business relationship through thick and thin, are we? After all, business decisions are made with a different set of criteria, with your eye always on the bottom line. You have to be ruthless sometimes to make a good business decision. If you stick with a negative business relationship, you're asking for trouble.

One of the realities of the network marketing paradigm is that the line between 'personal' and 'business' is blurred. Many times, the first people you introduce to the opportunity are your friends and family. Maybe they're people you go to church with or people from your neighborhood. The traditional business paradigm insists on separating your business life and your personal life, and sometimes that's understandable. After all, it's hard to know how some people would live with themselves if they couldn't shrug off responsibility for their actions by saying, "That was just business." In network marketing, you have a responsibility to the people you introduce to the opportunity. You cannot separate your personal values from your business ethics. You cannot hide behind the idea of the 'company' – you take responsibility for your own actions. Of course, you also benefit from your actions in a way that isn't possible in the traditional paradigm.

THE CORE VALUES

THE PRINCIPLES THAT underlie a strong relationship are embodied in the four Core Values: *freedom, equality, worth of the individual,* and *love.*

In 1995, I recorded an audiotape titled "The Core Values" and distributed it throughout the Nutrition For Life organization. Today, everyone who starts a Nutrition For Life business receives a copy of this tape. It is more than a corporate statement – it represents truths that have guided this industry from the beginning. I claim no credit for 'inventing' these values, or even identifying them. All I did was look at the strongest business relationships in our industry and ask, "What's at the foundation?"

When people leave the traditional paradigm and come to network marketing, they are looking for something. On the one hand, they want to achieve a state of being or level of achievement that wasn't open to them before. On the other hand, they want an environment in which they can express things they couldn't express before. They want the freedom to be themselves and the security you need to live free. It's a tall order, but through network marketing many people have achieved exactly that.

In the past, I've always tried to emphasize the practical side of the Core Values. When you respect another person's freedom, treat them with equality and worth, and display genuine concern – even love – you do reap practical benefits. Machiavelli wrote that even though a prince may sometimes have to *act* immorally, he should always *seem* moral. My take is just the opposite. I've always thought that the only way to truly *seem* is to truly *be.* Don't waste time trying to look like you have character – act in accordance with principle and the 'seeming' will take care of itself. When you treat people right, they treat you right in return. The Golden Rule is still one of the most valuable principles of true achievement.

With all this emphasis on the practical side of principle, with this talk about reciprocity, it would be easy to think that the reason for living by principle is to be treated well by others. In fact, living by principle can often lead to the opposite effect. Freedom, equality, worth of the individual and love are not universally held principles, despite what people say. Sometimes it can be quite a challenge to keep these values front and center. After all, acknowledging another person's freedom can sometimes call our own freedom into question. Making allowances for what another person loves can lead to sacrifices when it comes to what we hold dear.

The nature of relationships demands that both partners gain and give. Each one goes out of his or her way to accommodate the other. Each one displays a respect for the other that allows for freedom, insures equality, affirms worth and displays love. Relationships can be challenging at times! – But they are also very strong.

FREEDOM

FREEDOM IS THE MOST OVER-USED WORD in the world today. So many things are justified in the name of 'freedom' that it boggles the mind. Freedom is a word we all *think* we understand, but you never really understand unless you've lived without it.

Nations have fought to protect and preserve our *political* freedom, but when it comes to *economic* freedom, we're on our own. Try as it might, no government can provide its citizens with true economic freedom. When Christ said, "The poor ye shall have with you always," he wasn't speaking metaphorically. No matter how sophisticated our society becomes, we are still faced with basic threats to our economic freedom. We are all vulnerable when it comes to our bank accounts.

The battle for financial freedom is one we fight alone. We spend eight hours a day on the battlefield, and even then, we're lucky to break even. Every major setback threatens to be a disaster. Is it any wonder that more and more people have given up on the traditional business paradigm and are looking for an alternative?

Part of the problem, of course, is that the traditional paradigm wasn't designed to give you freedom. Instead, individuals are grouped as commodities and put to work producing goods and services. The system is designed to create a profit for the owners and to keep the company itself thriving. The needs of the employee, even at the best firm, are secondary to those considerations. This isn't a value judgement. There's nothing inherently *wrong* with this system – just that it isn't a very effective one for achieving financial freedom.

After all, the average person works twenty years or more to earn retirement. During that time, the better part of each day is invested in someone else's gain. The worker is compensated not for his results, but for his time. The question is, after twenty years, is that all your time is worth?

The fact is, you determine the worth of your time by dictating what compensation you'll accept in return for it. Most of us set the price too low and live to regret it.

A friend once said: "In network marketing, the number one product we sell is freedom. Time freedom, financial freedom – that's what this business is really about."

I agree that the desire for freedom is one of the major factors drawing people to network marketing in the late twentieth century. That freedom takes as many shapes and forms as there are people to dream of it.

Political freedom is usually defined as the freedom *from* something: Freedom from tyranny, freedom from discrimination, freedom from taxation without representation. In contrast, economic freedom is usually thought of as the freedom *to do* something. If political freedom protects us, economic freedom acts as an enabling force. Today, as more and more people enjoy political freedom, it's natural that we yearn more and more for this new, enabling form of freedom.

Of all the Core Values, freedom is the easiest to characterize. Financial freedom lets you build your dream house, drive a new car, take a vacation, or send your kids to a good school. Financial freedom gives you power over circumstances and liberates you from debt and working two or more jobs to make ends meet. Financial freedom means being able to do things you never thought you'd be able to do – spending time where you choose, with the people you love.

Another form of freedom that is every bit as valuable but often goes unmentioned is the freedom to take control of your life. Most people spend their entire lives working on someone else's terms. Even if they love what they do, there are times when the job becomes a hard master. When you earn the freedom to take control of your life, you start setting your own priorities. You set your own pace. You don't have to build a wall between your personal life and your business life anymore.

FOCUS ON OTHERS

FREEDOM, EQUALITY, worth of the individual and love are all common ideas – ideas that need no explanation or definition. They are things we all feel strongly about, things we all desire in our personal and professional lives. We now know that deficiencies in these areas – particularly individual worth and love – can lead to serious consequences, so it comes as no surprise how important they are in a relationship.

As much as we cherish these values, it has to be said that our concern for them remains largely self-centered. By nature, we are much more sensitive to encroachments on our own freedom than we are to the limits we put on the freedom of those around us. We are far more aware of outside threats to our equality, or abuses of our love and worth, than we are of the threats we ourselves make on the equality, worth and love of others. In a sense, even the best of us are prone to hypocrisy, applying our ideals to how other people treat us much more rigorously than we examine our own treatment of them.

Our society is overburdened with complaints, to the extent that we have literally seen a devaluation of values. Once, we were taught values so that we could order our own behavior, temper our own conduct. Now, values are appropriated merely as areas of grievance, as measuring sticks of discrimination. We are much more willing to impose values on the rest of the world – an impossible feat – than to impose them on ourselves.

This reversal of order makes it necessary to point out that the Core Values are not a scale for measuring other people's treatment of us. Rather, they are a guide for structuring our treatment of others. The Core Values are not a list of merits we should seek to protect in ourselves, but rather a list of qualities we should seek to promote in our treatment of others. If you understand this, then the Core Values become a very powerful tool for creating strong reciprocal relationships with other people.

Let's consider an example. We'll use the idea of 'freedom' since we've talked about it already. When we think of freedom in the context of relationships, we tend to think of freedom being constrained. One of the classic reasons people avoid relationships – both romantic and professional – is the fear of incurring an obligation that will curb their freedom of action. By nature we want to conserve our freedom, to avoid having our actions dictated by necessity. We are extremely cautious in relationships because we know instinctively that a strong relationship involves a curtailment of freedom.

A familiar example in terms of romantic relationships is the image of the confirmed bachelor commiserating with the new husband, pointing out all the things he is no longer free to do now that he has a wife. The irony is, the husband doesn't feel the loss of freedom. In fact, his options seem much more open than they did before he married the girl he loved. For the bachelor, the relationship represents an infringement of freedom. For the new husband, the relationship is an enabling force – actually creating freedom that was never there before. Of course, on the surface, his bachelor friend is right: he has taken on certain obligations where his wife is concerned. But the husband made a conscious decision to sacrifice these small freedoms in return for a larger one. The relationship, while it has closed some doors, has opened many others.

What I'm trying to illustrate here is that there are two very different ways of looking at relationships, and they depend on who you focus on. When you focus on yourself, you become sensitive to your own freedom and wary of any limits that may be placed on it. When you focus on someone else, you look for ways to increase and enhance their freedom, even, sometimes, at the expense of your own. This focus on others, while it closes a few doors, opens many, many more.

In network marketing, one of the areas you can see this truth demonstrated is in the way we sponsor new people into the opportunity. Some people are pressured into looking at the opportunity, while others are allowed to choose. The outlook of the person introducing them determines the difference. If that person is focused on himself, he will create pressure to respond. Adding another distributor to his sales organization will increase his freedom, and increasing his own freedom is what he's focused on. So, he feels justified in applying pressure in order to control the decision-making process.

A sponsor who focuses on the freedom of the prospect instead of focusing on his or her own freedom, will understand that by attempting to control the decision, a sponsor takes freedom from the prospect. That loss of freedom results in poor decisions – even if the prospect decides to start their own network marketing business, the commitment to seeing it grow will be weak. So, a sponsor who focuses on other people's freedom will adopt a 'pressure-free' approach to prospecting.

The best decisions are made in the context of a relationship where a person's freedom, equality, worth and love are all respected and preserved. Only in such a relationship can people feel good about their decisions and stick with it through thick and thin. In other words, a relationship that preserves and promotes the Core Values is a breeding ground of lasting commitment.

EQUALITY

SOME PEOPLE DON'T THINK of you as an equal. Before they can accord you with the honor of being treated as an equal, they feel you need to prove yourself. You've run into these people before – you can probably spot them right away. And, try as you might, you probably have a difficult time respecting them, because you know that, deep down, they don't respect you.

We like to classify things and group them according to magnitude. By nature, we are organizers, and sometimes we fall into the trap of organizing people. One of the most persistent downfalls of human society has been the urge to rank people according to worth. Even today, many cultures that now enjoy political freedom are still tarnished with the vestiges of a class system – a declaration that people are inherently unequal.

On a social level, this tendency is nothing more than a reflection of how we often behave in our personal lives. For whatever reason, we conclude that some types of people are better than others, and we make decisions based on this conclusion. If you think about it, all complaints of discrimination are essentially protests against decisions based on the notion of inherent inequality.

Another brand of inequality that has plagued history is the inequality of opportunity. Some people have a head start over others. Some people have more opportunities open to them than others do. It's easy to say that 'achievers create their own opportunities,' but the fact is, life isn't fair. Some people do have an advantage when it comes to opportunity. In life, there are few level playing fields, and there is very little any of us can do to change this.

If this weren't the case – if things were really fair – it wouldn't matter if some people mistakenly perpetuated inequalities. We could dismiss their view and get on with life, knowing that people really are equal. Unfortunately, inequalities do exist. That's why it is so important to elevate equality as a Core Value, as an idea to be actively promoted within relationships.

You see, equality is not a state of being. Equality is something we create with our actions and attitudes. When we actively promote the value of equality in relationships, we enable other people to take advantage of opportunities they might not otherwise enjoy. We also help build their sense of worth. If you've ever wondered what you can do to make the world a better place – what you, with your limited influence can do to make a difference – then, listen carefully: promote equality in all your relationships and you will literally change people's lives.

I wasn't born to a wealthy family. I was the youngest boy in a large family and although we got by, we were by no means well off. We lived in a small house, and I got used to wearing hand-me-downs from my older brothers. As far as material advantages went, I didn't enjoy very many. Fortunately, my parents gave me a gift much greater than that – the gift of character. As I grew older, it seemed there was always someone there to promote my best interest, to see that I was treated fairly and had access to opportunities. I consider myself to have been extremely blessed. At the same time, I know that in many ways my case was exceptional. I've met people who started off with many of the advantages I lacked, but never had the kind of support and encouragement I received. I am convinced that the enabling power of strong relationships is much more important than any material advantage you can enjoy. Wealth without relationships is nothing.

You can help other people in many ways. The most obvious form of assistance is charity – the donation of money and time to help those less fortunate. Charity is a noble thing, an essential way of 'giving back' to the community that has helped you prosper. But many people are not in a position to give money to worthy causes – they have pressing needs of their own to meet. Even so, there is something more valuable than money that we all have the power – and the responsibility to give – and that is *opportunity*.

Your network marketing business actually provides you with an unlimited supply of opportunity to share with others. And it's a unique kind of opportunity, too. It's an *equal* opportunity in the best sense of the word. Anyone can do it. No one lacks the necessary qualifications. No matter what your background is, you can duplicate the success of others in network marketing.

I, for one, never expected to be able to share an opportunity with other people. Like most of us, I spent my time *looking* for opportunities. I fixed myself firmly on the receiving end and waited to see what would come my way. All that changed when I began my network marketing business, because suddenly it was in my self-interest to share the opportunity with other people. By helping other people start their own businesses, I was actually expanding my own.

At first, I confess that I didn't share the opportunity with everyone. No, I was looking for a certain kind of person, someone who would create an overnight sensation. At that point, I was looking for 'hares' and letting 'tortoises' fend for themselves.

In my early days as a network marketer, I started to remember some of the lessons I'd learned in college when I had a job in a retail men's clothing store. My old boss, Mr. Al Levine, passed on all kinds of wisdom from decades in the business. One of the things he taught me was how important it was for each salesman to pull his weight. He scrutinized everything I said to customers, and he critiqued me later. He set a high standard for me and the other guys to reach – a standard that sometimes generated healthy competition between us. After a few months working for Mr.Levine, each one of us was a high-performance selling enthusiast. Customers walked out of our store carrying bags over their shoulders, boxes under their arms, and they were a whole lot lighter in the billfold.

When I started sharing the opportunity with other people, I thought I needed a group of high performance salespeople like the ones I'd worked with in college. I knew exactly what I was looking for, and I knew there weren't many around. I went to great lengths to spot them and give them my presentation – and a few of them agreed to give it a try. As far as I was concerned, I was putting together a powerhouse organization by choosing only the best people.

Along the way, I also introduced some others who seemed less suited to the task. I didn't discourage them, but I also didn't spend a lot of time working with them. Instead, I focused on my stars, my great salespeople, the ones I knew would perform.

Over time, a funny thing happened. Some of my 'hares' decided to stop for a nap. Now that they were on their own, without a manager pushing them to perform, they decided to take it easy. They were still enthusiastic, and they still paid lip service to the business, but they just slacked off and stopped doing anything. At the same time, some of my 'tortoises' were making headway. The people I had written off, the people I had never really *wanted* on my team, became some of the best achievers. The realization finally hit me: I had been judging my prospects with an obsolete standard. Instead of treating them equally, I had put my efforts into helping the ones who had been most successful in the traditional paradigm – the ones who had benefited most from the old way of doing things, and therefore had less to gain by changing their thinking. Meanwhile, the people who had never impressed me in the traditional setting were duplicating my performance – even *surpassing* it! – in the new paradigm. Let me tell you, that got me thinking.

No matter how qualified you feel, you are in no position to judge how other people will respond to opportunity. The only sensible approach to building your own business is to treat others with a true sense of equality. Give people an equal chance to learn about the opportunity – treat them as if you think they can do it – and you'll be surprised by some of the people who rise to the occasion.

WORTH OF THE INDIVIDUAL

MOST PEOPLE DO NOT REALIZE what they have within them. They have no idea what they could really accomplish if put to the test. It's very rare to find a person with a good sense of their individual worth. For the majority of us, self-worth and self-esteem are highly problematic. We go from one extreme to another – sometimes trusting ourselves fully and doubting ourselves completely the next moment.

As with most people, this is a challenging topic for me to deal with. I have a good idea of my shortcomings and weaknesses, and I have to admit that they sometimes seem to overshadow my strengths. For everything I think I do well, there are a dozen things I have my doubts about. And I'm not alone.

Today, problems related to low self-esteem are on the rise. One of the topics I'm asked about most in the context of successful business building is the role of self-esteem. People have a hard time believing they are *capable* of making it. They are so conscious of their failings and so blind to everything but the strengths of their mentors that they just can't conceive of following in their role models' footsteps.

One of the most valuable pieces of advice I've ever read was found in Peter Drucker's book, *The Effective Executive*. In a number of books, Drucker writes persuasively about the need to build on our strengths rather than compensating for our weaknesses. Chapter 4 of *The Effective Executive* is titled 'Making Strength Productive,' and here Drucker compares the staffing strategies of the Union and Confederate armies during the U.S. Civil War:

President Lincoln, when told that General Grant, his new commander-in-chief, was fond of the bottle said:

'If I knew his brand, I'd send a barrel or so to some other generals.' After childhood on the Kentucky and Illinois frontier, Lincoln assuredly knew all about the bottle and its dangers. But of all the Union generals, Grant alone had proven consistently capable of planning and leading winning campaigns. Grant's appointment was the turning point of the Civil War. It was an effective appointment because Lincoln chose his general for his tested ability to win battles and not for his sobriety, that is, for the absence of a weakness.

Lincoln learned this the hard way however. Before he chose Grant, he had appointed in succession three or four Generals whose main qualifications were their lack of major weaknesses. As a result, the North, despite its tremendous superiority in men and matériel, had not made any headway for three long years from 1861 to 1864. In sharp contrast, Lee, in command of the Confederate forces, had staffed from strength. Every one of Lee's generals, from Stonewall Jackson on, was a man of obvious and monumental weaknesses. But these failings Lee considered – rightly – to be irrelevant. Each of them had, however, one area of real strength – and it was this strength, and only this strength, that Lee utilized and made effective. As a result, the "well-rounded" men Lincoln had appointed were beaten time and again by Lee's 'single-purpose tools,' the men of narrow but very great strength.

The lesson here is simple: Your value as an achiever is not a matter of eliminating or even compensating for your weaknesses. Instead, success is a matter of building your strengths.

We sometimes forget that the people whose success we wish to emulate are as human and fallible as we are. As a rule, people do not advance because they are good at everything. They advance because they are very good at one thing. To get where you want to be, you don't have to master a complex process. You don't have to become an expert on the millions of nuances that combine to create the human psyche. You just have to find one thing you're strong at and build that strength.

Individual worth is not contingent on performance or even nature. In my opinion, individual worth is grounded in *potential*. Each individual has great worth because each individual has vast potential. I believe that to achieve greatness, you don't have to transform yourself into someone else. You just have to find out who you can be and become that person. The way to do that is to find your strengths and increase them.

In a relationship, you have the ability to awaken people to their true potential. One of the things that makes mentors so valuable is the way they can open us up to what we have the potential to become. Every dream is really an expression of what we would like to be. When a person tells you her dream is to drive a Mercedes or put a swimming pool in her back yard, it doesn't mean she's a 'materialist.' When people dream of 'things,' what they're usually saying is, "I want to grow into the kind of person who has this thing." Dreams must be understood as an expression of potential. Which means that you, through relationships, give people the encouragement to make their dreams a reality.

The more skeptical among us think that dreams are little more than wishful thinking. I disagree. If you deny the power of dreams, you deny an individual's ability to reach his or her full potential. We all have dreams, and very few of our dreams are truly outside the realm of possibility. The skeptics are fond of pointing out that the little boy who dreams of becoming an astronaut doesn't have much chance to succeed at it. I don't dispute that. On the other hand, that same little boy dreams of growing up to be like his dad, to make people proud of him, to be a hero to the girl he loves. Are these things beyond the realm of possibility? Of course not. Most dreams are precisely of this nature. They express our inner longing to reach our true potential. A person who denies the power of dreams is fighting a losing battle, considering how many of his own childhood dreams have already come true!

We are all worthy of having our dreams come true. The process by which they become a reality is the process by which we come to fulfill our potential – as we build up our strengths, we get closer to our dreams.

The idea of 'worth' is really a measure of value, and value is by no means a fixed quantity. Value shifts over time, and it is linked inextricably with potential. A seed has value in the sense that it has the potential to blossom. An investment has value in the sense that it has potential to earn a dividend. An individual has value both inherently and in the sense that he or she has the potential to achieve great things. Through relationships, you have the power to awaken people to this potential, and that is an ability of great value in itself.

LOVE

LOVE IS THE MOST IMPRECISE – and therefore the most versatile – word in our language. Love is a word whose meaning is defined by its context, a tone of voice, or the setting in which it is uttered. To speak of love and business in the same breath seems to some people to be an expression of weakness.

Of course, I disagree. Think of it this way: You will spend most of your waking hours engaged in some kind of work, in return for some form of compensation. The kind of work you do represents a huge commitment. In many contexts, we define ourselves by our profession. For better or worse, we invest most of our time and energy and creativity into the work we do. Now if that's the case, it seems to me that the only way to justify this kind of commitment is to love the work you do.

Love is another one of those things modern society wants us to keep at home. Don't bring your feelings to work. To be a productive member of society, you've got to keep your personal life and your work separate. If anything, you can comfort yourself with the knowledge that you are working to put food on the table. I am amazed at some of the things we justify because we have to work. Our children grow up before we know it, our spouses lead independent lives, our friends and family see us infrequently and only for quick glimpses. In fact, we don't really have friends outside of work anymore – just about everyone we know is someone we work with.

The economic factors which have combined to make this a reality are too complex to analyze here, but I think it's safe to say that we all realize that in the traditional business paradigm, the people we love and the work we do are two separate, often competing things. One of the ways network marketing can make a difference in people's lives is by putting their personal and professional lives back together.

Love begins with a genuine concern for other people. In a sense, relationships are impossible without some form of love. If you don't care about what happens to another person, you can't really enter a relationship with them – even a business relationship. In fact, I've sometimes been surprised to discover a relationship between me and another person that I didn't realize existed, all because I found myself concerned about what they were doing, or realized they were concerned about me. Mutual concern is a sign of a strong relationship.

At Nutrition For Life, we think of ourselves as the protector of our distributors' dreams. Many of the things we do internally are motivated by the desire to add stability to distributor businesses or to help them expand. These initiatives are nothing more than expressions of the concern we have for the success of people who start Nutrition For Life businesses – a sign of the relationship we have with them.

One of the things about love that makes it so important in a relationship is that, at its best, love is unconditional. Relationships are reciprocal in the sense that each party assists and supports the other, but they are not contingent on that support and assistance. In other words, relationships persist no matter how the parties involved respond. Your concern for another person doesn't wane because he or she wasn't able to assist you with a project or meet you at an event. These circumstances remain on the surface without troubling the deeper solidity of the bond.

You might say, "What about a bad relationship?" Well, there's no question that bad relationships exist. There are situations in business where one person takes all the benefit without giving any in return. I know first hand how disappointing these relationships can be, but rather than contradicting the rule, I think they reinforce it. You see, if you remain true to the values that underlie the relationship, your conduct is above reproach. You can't speak for another person's conduct, but you are responsible for you own. One of the most dangerous notions alive today is the idea that one person's bad behavior justifies an equally bad response. Today, we tend to think nothing of 'stooping' to that level, and that's a shame. We should be more concerned with our own conduct, which we have the power to control, than with the conduct of others, which we cannot control and – in all honesty – are in no position to judge.

The number one argument against 'love' in the context of business is that it opens you up to being taken advantage of. I have to admit this is the case. I don't claim to hold many world records, but I believe I am definitely in the running for 'most taken advantage of.'

Why? Because I try to act in good faith, and I believe in second chances. Sometimes people who have fewer scruples can take advantage of that – and sometimes I catch myself thinking, "I've got to start trusting people less!" Then, I realize what I've just said and I have to shake my head. Trust people less? What kind of a way is that to build a relationship?

For every person who takes advantage of your trust, you'll find ten who respond to it and become lifelong friends. For every person who uses their relationship with you unfairly, you'll find ten who value their relationship with you more than anything. For every person who treats you badly, you'll earn the lasting respect of ten who are eminently worthy of it.

Machiavelli, the guru of slash-and-burn business writers, believed that, for a man in office, it is better to be feared than to be loved. I know a lot of people who still subscribe to this notion – they believe that power, not principle, is the foundation of all relationships. If you try to convince them otherwise, they fall back on the saying, 'Nice guys finish last.' If you trust people and seek their love, they'll only stab you in the back. Well, you know what? We *all* get stabbed in the back at one point or another. The difference is, people who base their relationships on love have friends to turn to, and people who put their trust in fear are unmourned and on their own.

My good friend Dayle Maloney's book, *I Could Have Quit $7,000,000.00 Ago!* is subtitled: 'Proof – Nice Guys Do Finish First!' What an inspiration! Dayle, who has worked so hard on behalf of so many different people and helped make so many dreams come true, is one of the most trusting men I know. He has gotten involved with people no one else believed in, and helped make them successful. Why? Because he believes in people, and he wants to see them reach their potential. In all the years I've known him, Dayle has always been an example of how love works in business. When that man gets up on stage, people give him a standing ovation; not because he's a great speaker (although he is) but because he's touched so many of their lives. In other words, they love him. Has Dayle been taken advantage of over the years? Sure he has. Oddly enough, it doesn't seem to have cramped his style – and it certainly hasn't prevented his success.

Remember, we all tend to focus on ourselves. We take ourselves too seriously, we look out for ourselves too much. One of the things I've noticed about myself is that I make it my business to look out for people I care about. We all do. Now, if people care about me, that means they'll look out for my interests, even when I'm not around. That's one of the advantages of relationships we often fail to consider – the more relationships you build, the more people are looking out for your best interests. If you stop and consider the implications of this, you'll see just how powerful relationships can really be.

A FRAMEWORK OF VALUES

MAKING A DIFFERENCE is what happens when you practice values in making a living. The importance of the Core Values to your success in business and in life cannot be overstated. One of the reasons why so many people have become disillusioned with the traditional business paradigm is that it's an environment in which living by principle doesn't always work. The thing that sets network marketing apart – the thing that makes me so proud of this industry and all it has accomplished – is that here, we have created an environment where living by principles is not only right but *effective*. We've discovered a venture where doing the right thing makes good business sense.

In this chapter, we've looked at the importance of relationships and the role values play in making them work. In a few pages, we've covered a lot of ground. To digest this information and apply it to your life, there are a few things you'll need to do:

1. LEARN THE CORE VALUES

When we talk about abstract ideas like freedom, equality, worth of the individual, and love, it's easy to get confused. It's not enough to learn the names, you've got to absorb the ideas, too. Take some time out and review this chapter. Learn the names *and* the ideas. Using the examples I've given, look for expressions of these values in your everyday life, in relationships you already have. Look for ways that other people have encouraged your sense of freedom, equality, worth and love. Also, think of times when you encouraged these traits in others. By thinking of specific examples, you will take these abstract ideas and give them concrete meaning in your life.

2. MAKE THE VALUES YOUR OWN

You can't live according to someone else's values. Until you take ownership of the Core Values, you won't be able to encourage them effectively in relationships. The Core Values are not specialized concepts – we all understand them and believe in them. Even so, you need to accept them as appropriate in a business setting. If you've always kept your personal and professional lives separate, this could take some getting used to. You may be willing to promote the Core Values in personal relationships, but reluctant to be so open in business dealings. If so, I encourage you do some soul searching, to really consider the potential of ideas like these applied in your professional life. Then, make the Core Values truly your own. Start practicing them and promoting them in your relationships with other people. They really will make a difference.

3. EXAMINE YOUR RELATIONSHIPS

Take a good look at the foundation of your current business relationships. Are these relationships really working? Do you feel that there is a bond of trust already in place, or do you have misgivings? Consider specific relationships and ask yourself, "What would happen here if I put their concerns ahead of mine?" Be honest, too. It's perfectly possible that some of your relationships could result in you being taken advantage of. Give that some thought – what is the 'worst case scenario'? Remember, you can't change relationships overnight, and you may be involved in relationships that would be better left untouched. Some relationships could actually be weaknesses – things you can't improve or eliminate. Don't worry about that. Instead, focus on relationships that are already strong and consider what would happen if you made them even stronger. The purpose of this step is to take a realistic inventory of your relationships and the values they're built on. Only then can you begin to make changes.

4.   BUILD A FRAMEWORK OF VALUES

I recommend a specific method of incorporating the Core Values into your life. Convert each value into it's own question, and use these questions to evaluate your actions within the relationship. *What can I do to increase his or her sense of freedom? How can I treat him or her with more equality? How can I encourage him or her to fulfill their potential worth? How can I show my concern?* These are the types of questions that create a positive framework of values. The emphasis is not on what you will receive, but on what you can do. Every relationship will benefit you in a different and unpredictable way. By operating within a framework of values, you provide a consistent impetus to building the relationship – a force that focuses on the other person's well being. Archimedes said he could move the world if you gave him a lever and a place to stand. Your relationships are your lever, and your values are the foundation you stand on.

CHAPTER THREE
The Culture of Achievement

IN THE 1960s, a growing number of young people became dissatisfied with the prevailing culture and created what came to be known as the 'counter-culture.' Unlike a sub-culture, which is a specialized facet of the culture at large, a counter-culture finds fault with the mainstream and attempts to create an alternative way of life. Today, society is inundated by would-be counter-cultures – although many of them are truly only radical offshoots of the culture at large.

Some people believe that network marketing is a sub-culture of marketing, a variant distribution method. On the surface this is true. Many of the techniques developed in traditional marketing can be adapted for use in network marketing. Many of the ideas and methods can also be assimilated. The original concept behind network marketing was a variation on 'word of mouth' advertising. Rather than promoting products through the media, companies could promote them through individual distributors, people with first-hand experience of the product's benefit who were trusted by their customers. Instead of spending millions of dollars to create a friendly face for the corporation, the independent distributor would serve as the conduit between the manufacturer and the consumer.

Considered from the corporate perspective, you could say that networking is a marketing strategy not unlike any other strategy and therefore a sub-set or sub-culture of marketing in general. From the point of view of the independent distributor, things look quite different.

I should know. I didn't start out on the corporate side of network marketing. I began as an independent distributor. I didn't know anything about marketing except what I'd learned as a part-time salesman during college. I didn't know anything about corporations. When I started my network marketing business, I wanted a good part-time income to supplement what I was making as a teacher. I had no idea where this new career path would eventually lead.

No matter how it looks from the ivory tower, network marketing is not a sub-culture of the traditional business paradigm. I learned that right away. There was something very different going on here, something that wasn't happening anywhere else I'd ever been. Network marketing was, if anything, a counter-culture. The ideas and methods I practiced were against the grain. In my more radical moments, I imagined myself a crusader against the nine-to-five world, replacing time cards with time freedom at a flick of the wrist.

One of the things I discovered as I got further into my network marketing career was, I needed something to sustain me, some source of new ideas and inspiration to keep me focused and tuned in to my goals. I wasn't getting that kind of input from the outside world. My fellow teachers were a little shocked at what I was doing. While they were at home relaxing after a day at school, I was hustling over to meetings, meeting people, networking. They mowed the lawn on Saturdays while I hopped into the car and went prospecting. My peers didn't offer their support – although they *did* offer to talk some sense into me. Even when I was making money, they didn't seem to be impressed.

My fellow distributors were an encouragement, but most of them had been in the business no longer than I had. They knew the challenges I faced, but they didn't have any answers. If I was going to find a source of training and inspiration, I would have to look elsewhere.

I've always been a believer in the power of good books. I soaked up all the business books I could get my hands on – Dale Carnegie, Zig Ziglar, Napoleon Hill. I attended all the sales training seminars I could find and did everything I could to adapt the lessons of traditional business to network marketing. In a sense, I created my very own counter-culture of success, filling my mind with great ideas and new inspiration every time I opened a book.

If you learn only one lesson from reading *Making A Difference*, let it be this: *to create a business that lasts, you've got to remove yourself from the traditional business culture and plug in to the culture of achievement.*

THE POWER OF CULTURE

WE ARE ALL, to one extent or another, products of our culture. Experts argue back and forth over the degree of influence our environment has, but we all agree that culture exerts a significant pull on us. Our ideas and beliefs are shaped, in part, by our culture. Our sense of what's proper and decent is influenced by the world around us. Our manners and customs are dictated almost entirely by culture. Another factor influenced by culture is our sense of what is possible.

"It won't work" is a well-documented response to network marketing opportunities. We all have stories we could share. After showing the plan, we are accosted by a person who insists on explaining why the plan won't work. No matter what argument we put forward (the fact that we are successful, the fact that other people have been successful), the man responds with, "I'll tell you why it won't work." You just can't get through to the guy, and unfortunately he's not alone. He's just one example of a type of person our culture produces in abundance: the non-achieving skeptic.

The non-achieving skeptic is convinced that he knows what's possible and what isn't. Judging from his track record, most things aren't possible. Under the same circumstances, you or I might wonder if maybe we were doing something wrong, but not this skeptic: he's convinced that what he can't do, no one can do. Interestingly enough, he doesn't even have to *try* something before he knows it's not possible. He knows it all instinctively.

Admittedly, we have a lot of fun at the skeptic's expense. After all, there is plenty of proof that network marketing works. Someone who denies it is revealing something about his or her own knowledge, not about the plan itself. Even so, it's important to understand that these skeptics embody a kind of logic that is deeply embedded in our mainstream culture.

Even though we pay lip service to entrepreneurs, our culture is highly suspicious of people who go out on their own and achieve success. We have certain notions about who should succeed, and how quickly they should succeed. We have definite ideas about how much a person should be able to make, and we can come down pretty hard if someone's earning 'too much.' Sympathy in our culture is with the *employee*, not the entrepreneur. Every aspect of society, from the tax code to the better business bureau, is engineered to discourage the entrepreneur. If you've ever wondered why over 80% of new businesses fail, it's because we live in a culture that undermines achievement.

A typical day at the office: Everyone gathers around the water cooler and commiserates. The company cuts back more and more people. The paychecks get smaller and smaller. The bills get bigger and bigger, and the kids demand more and more. What are we going to do? Well, did you hear about David? He started some kind of network marketing business. Oh, that won't work. Yeah, what a sucker. Well, let's get back to work.

How many people have this same conversation day after day? More and more people are fed up with their nine-to-five jobs. They want to find a way to reach more of their potential. They want their time and effort to add up to something more. And, oddly enough, they tear down anyone who does something about it! These are the worst kind of dream-stealers, because they want the same thing you do, but they're afraid. They just don't believe in their ability to succeed. And if they can't do it, well, neither can you.

You can't really blame them. They're acting out a pattern of thought that's been dictated by the culture. Entrepreneurs are special. We possess certain abilities the rest of the population just doesn't have. We're a rare breed. The majority of people are meant to work for someone else. That's the message we all hear in the workplace. At the same time entrepreneurs are praised, the praise is qualified by the warning that ordinary mortals need not apply. And, because so many people have such a low sense of individual worth (another by-product of our culture), they buy into it.

Then something strange happens. Somebody at the office, somebody just like us, thinks he can start his own business. The word circulates at the water cooler and we all wonder, "Who does he think he is?" After all, he's one of us. If one of us could be out there on our own, we'd already be doing it, right? Sometimes, the more 'concerned' among us will even have a chat with the wayward employee and try to talk some sense into him. That's what happened to me, and it will probably happen to you, too.

You see, your success as an independent distributor makes a statement that a lot of people aren't ready to accept: that 'regular' people can succeed in their own business. By starting your own network marketing business, you've put a hole in the myth that entrepreneurs are a breed apart – you've signaled to your co-workers that you think you can do it, too. And if you can do it – if you're willing to take the risk – why aren't they? That's a question they don't want to confront. The easy answer is, "It won't work."

Over the years, I've seen many different variations on this theme. In fact, one of the best parts of any network marketing success story is when the successful distributor shows up in the new car, or even quits the nine-to-five job, and the co-workers and neighbors and nay-sayers are left scratching their heads – or asking to get involved in the opportunity! The nay-sayers have been proven wrong time and time again by so many different people that it's hard to imagine anyone remaining skeptical. But they do.

And that skepticism can take its toll on your belief level. You see, a funny thing about ideas is that even the ones we know aren't true can have an impact on us if we hear them often enough. A good, if extreme, example is George Orwell's *1984* – if you hear it often enough, even though you know it's wrong, two plus two equals five. Negative ideas wear us down. They blunt our enthusiasm and, over time, make us passive. To remain successful outside the traditional paradigm, you need an antidote to the negative ideas, and that antidote is the culture of achievement.

CORRECTING THE CULTURE

CULTURE IS NOT A THING, it's a process. Our outlook on life is shaped, not by a single, vivid experience, but by a learning process that spans years. Many of the ideas we assimilate through this process are useful and necessary. Some are harmful. The culture of achievement does not replace mainstream culture. That would be too ambitious a task. Instead, it introduces a corrective view to the mainstream process, creating a new set of understandings and integrating them into the culture at large.

The mainstream culture teaches its lessons through passive participation. You learn through repetition and often as a by-product of some other activity. In contrast, the culture of achievement is an active process you initiate voluntarily for the express purpose of absorbing new information. This means that, while it is difficult if not impossible to withdraw from the mainstream culture, dropping out of the culture of achievement is as simple as reverting to passivity.

When my older son went to college, we thought he had perfect vision. He didn't wear glasses and seemed to do fine driving around our hometown in Louisiana. Then, I visited him at college. I rented a car and, one night, he took it for a spin in his new community. When he returned, the brakelights were shattered. "What happened?" I asked. "I backed into another car," he said. "I didn't see it." He also said that all the lights at night had seemed blurry and he couldn't see the lines that divided one lane from another. I didn't need to hear anything more: my son needed glasses.

After the optometrist measures your vision, you get a prescription. That prescription is essentially a formula for correcting your vision. You aren't seeing things clearly, but the answer isn't to replace your eyes. You just need a corrective device to bring things back into focus. The culture of achievement serves a similar function. It corrects the way you see things so that the facts aren't blurry anymore. Like glasses, the culture of achievement does not 'cure' the problem. As soon as you 'unplug,' it's as if you've left your glasses behind. Things are suddenly blurry again. That's how easy it is to drop out of the culture of achievement.

The culture of achievement consists of two parts: the *learning device*, and *the process of using it*. Learning devices come in many forms, but they consist primarily of books, audiotapes, training seminars, videos, meetings, rallies and special educational tools. When these learning tools are used systematically, they counteract the negative messages of the mainstream culture and build support for new, achievement-oriented thinking. The culture of achievement, then, is a form of continuing education whose aim is to help you achieve and maintain personal and professional success.

As a former teacher, I have always put a lot of faith in the power of education. In life, you never really leave school. The learning process is continual and inevitable. Given this, you would expect people to know twice as much at the age of forty as they did at the age of twenty. Sadly, the learning process – like the culture of achievement – is not passive. It yields the greatest dividends to those who make the more serious commitments. If you want to learn the lessons of success, you've got to pursue them actively. You have to search them out, put them to the test, and make them your own.

Teachers have known for a long time that certain topics outside the traditional scope of education can be taught using its tools. In the nineteenth and early twentieth centuries, a significant literature developed whose aim was to help develop character in its readers. The theory was that be exposing young people to character-building books (not one book, by the way, but a whole series of them), you would stimulate and nurture character in them. Did it work? Yes, it did, and books like this were in use until quite recently, when 'character' fell out of favor in certain circles.

In network marketing, this theory was adapted to create the culture of achievement. Early on in the history of this industry, people realized that independent distributors needed some kind of support structure to help them succeed. They were, after all, swimming against the current. Perhaps a series of the right kind of books could help develop a 'successful' character in people who committed themselves to the process of reading them.

Over the years, the learning devices and the processes for using them have become more and more sophisticated. The development of the culture of achievement reached an all-time high in 1995, when Nutrition For Life introduced a monthly training and personal development supplement which included books, audiotapes, and even video presentations. Since that time, a number of other programs have emerged attempting to duplicate the success of the program. Although none has yet replicated its success, they all point to the continued effectiveness of company-sponsored training programs as transmission tools for the culture of achievement.

UNDERSTANDING THE PROCESS

TO GET A BETTER UNDERSTANDING of the cultural process, let's look at the monthly training program as an example. This program combined two features which many network marketing organizations had already introduced – 'book-of-the-month' and 'tape-of-the-month' clubs – and added a third element: an integrated training supplement that made the material on the book and tapes applicable to the practical process of network marketing.

Books, of course, were the time-honored tools of self-development. As long as books have been written, authors have shared their knowledge in an attempt to help the reader improve his or her understanding. In fact, until recently, the process of learning and the process of reading were virtually synonymous. Books are undoubtedly the most convenient tools for education: they are portable, require no electricity, and they can be studied again and again. A good library of 'success books' is the repository of untold wisdom.

Cassette tapes revolutionized the training process in every field of endeavor. With cassette tapes, you could attend lectures behind the wheel of your car! Network marketers immediately realized the effectiveness of the cassette tape as a training tool. Unlike books, which required years of study and preparation, a cassette tape could be made quickly and inexpensively. It also allowed a certain level of passive learning – you could listen to it while doing something else and still absorb at least some of the message. As compact cassette players become universal, the audiotape came into its own as a training device. Now, you could develop a successful new outlook on business while you jogged in the park or drove to work. They made great tools for introducing others to the opportunity, too – you could pass them out to everyone you knew.

Books can be an excellent source of visual and abstract information. Cassette tapes provide the necessary auditory component. With the introduction of video, the arsenal was complete. Combined, these tools allow the creation of something that a generation ago would have been impossible – an alternative learning culture, a culture that focuses not on conformity and mediocrity but on outstanding achievement.

Because culture is a process, it wasn't enough to put together one training package. The natural tendency when you create a training tool is to want to cover every single possibility. You want to pack all the information you have into one massive tool. Unfortunately, a single tool, no matter how good it is, does not make a process. A much more effective approach is to divide up the information and serve it in smaller, more manageable pieces, a new one each month.

One of the hallmarks of the mainstream culture is a phenomenon we call 'information overload.' The culture saturates its participants with more information than they can use, forcing them to pick and choose what to adopt and what to ignore. Many theorists have criticized this effect, attributing all kinds of negative effects to it. I take a different view. Information 'overload' is something we've always had as part of the learning process. I can't think of a single class I ever took that didn't overload me with more information than I could reasonably remember, understand and apply. Rather than crippling my ability to learn, this overload sent a valuable message. It said: "There is much more to learn than you realize – keep going." That was the message that let me know I had to stay plugged in and keep on learning. If you don't experience information overload, you aren't getting enough information!

Although the monthly training program was designed to develop sensitivity and awareness in network marketers, it had an unexpected by-product: many of its users reported experiencing benefits not only in their network marketing businesses but in their nine-to-five jobs, too. The principles they absorbed by participating in the culture of achievement were transforming their performance in the traditional paradigm, a testament to the power of education if ever there was one.

THE HUMAN FACTOR

BOOKS AND TAPES do not a culture make. As effective as they are in communicating ideas, books and tapes alone do not complete the cultural process. If learning is the goal of the process, *personal interaction* provides the catalyst. The 'human factor' provides the environment where the lessons from books and tapes take root.

A network marketing opportunity meeting is one of the most unusual get-togethers you will ever attend. It combines the intensity of a sporting event with the enthusiasm of an old-fashioned church meeting. I've never found anything that reproduces the same level of energy and excitement, the same emotional outlet. I love meetings, what can I say?

I'll never forget my first meeting. It felt like a gathering of some kind of secret society. I was pretty nervous. The only person I really knew was my sponsor, and I was fairly shy around new people. The thing that made it so fascinating, though, was the fact that the other people there were doing the same thing I was. Like me, they had decided to enter this unique, sometimes mysterious world of network marketing.

Before that night, I thought I believed in the opportunity. If you'd have asked me, I would have said there was nothing you could do to get me more excited, because I was at the peak. I had no idea what was in store.

The thing that makes the event so thrilling isn't what's happening on stage – although that can be pretty exciting. Instead, it's what's happening in the audience, in you and in the people around you. There's this incredible sense of shared purpose. After spending so much time in the outside world, where no one is doing what you're doing, it's a shock to suddenly be surrounded by colleagues, people who know exactly what you're up to and agree completely. The validation you receive is priceless. I remember looking around the room at all the well-dressed professional-looking people and thinking, "If that guy's involved in this, I must have made the right choice,"

"Wow, those two look successful," and "Oh my goodness – is that a *real* Rolex?" Yes, it was an experience I will never forget.

Today, we live in a world of separation. We guard our privacy. We don't know our neighbors and don't want to know them. The thought of driving three hours to spend the evening with a hundred committed network marketing distributors can be a little daunting. Meeting new people, trying to remember all those names, trying to say the right thing all the time – can't I just stick with my books and tapes?

The human factor is the catalyst that makes the books and tapes worthwhile. Without the human factor, the belief you derive from training and motivational tools is only on loan. It's at the meetings and functions that you take possession of the new ways of thinking and permanently elevate your belief level. I don't have any medical research to back me, but I wouldn't be surprised to learn that network marketing events help your body secrete a 'success enzyme' that boosts your belief level sky high!

RECOGNITION

MEETINGS AND EVENTS are also the venue for one of the most important parts of the culture of achievement: *recognition*. Somewhere I have a trophy I received in the late 1970s singling me out as my organization's top performer. On top of the trophy is a golden businessman wearing a suit and tie, carrying a little briefcase. Now, I haven't always carried a briefcase (I've never worn a golden suit, for that matter), but receiving that trophy was one of the proudest moments in my life as a distributor.

In the nine-to-five world, people scratch and claw for recognition. Recognition is so powerful that people are often willing to trade pay raises and other perks in return for it. Some corporations have developed programs that substitute recognition for increased compensation – and the programs work! The desire to be singled out as an achiever is so powerful that people will do all sorts of things to get it.

The problem is, in the nine-to-five world, there's a pervasive belief that recognition is not handed out according to merit. As the desire for recognition mounts, people who lack recognition become more and more convinced that the ground rules are unfair. Excellent performance isn't enough – it all depends on who you know.

When recognition is separated from performance, it becomes a subjective measure, not of who is best, but of who is most appreciated. When this happens, recognition actually backfires on the people who give it because it tells other performers that their work is *not* appreciated. And these achievers, even when they're satisfied with their work and salary, are leaving in larger and larger numbers for this very reason.

At the heart of the 'recognition crisis' in the traditional business paradigm is the sense people have that they are not reaching their full potential. A surprising number of top level managers in corporate America believe their positions do not take full advantage of what they have to offer. Despite their success, they are willing to leave the corporate world behind in search of new challenges, all because they're seeking a form of recognition that is purely based on the merits of their performance – a recognition that measures them at their best.

The popularity of recognition in network marketing stems from the fact that it provides precisely what is missing in the corporate world: an unbiased performance-based recognition of achievement.

In network marketing, the performance standards are clear. Each level of achievement is delineated, corresponding to a level of compensation (the fact that compensation and performance are directly linked is another attractive feature of network marketing). To get the recognition, you perform to the standard. It's that simple, and it relies entirely on your own ability.

Every once in awhile, someone will ask, "Why do you let *that* person be so successful in your organization?" The person asking generally has some sort of grievance, real or imagined, against the distributor in question. My answer is simple: "I don't *let* people succeed. They *earn* their success, and I make sure they're recognized for it." You see, none of Nutrition For Life's thousands of distributors works for me. Each of them is independent – self-employed. Unlike a traditional business, where the boss elevates the people he prefers, in my company, the top performers are elevated and there is no 'boss' to make his preferences known. It's a system of recognition that is blind to every consideration but achievement.

That's why recognition in network marketing is such an honor. Everyone in the organization has the opportunity to achieve recognition, and everyone knows the criteria. When you accept recognition of achievement, everyone knows and appreciates exactly what you had to do to get it. In addition, everyone who hasn't already achieved this performance level knows that you are a role model to follow. You see, there is no competition for recognition in network marketing. Any achiever can earn it, and then become an example for others to emulate.

THE THEORY OF ACTION

BEFORE WE LEAVE the culture of achievement, let me explain what I call the 'theory of action' – the psychology behind making a successful transition from the traditional business paradigm to the new paradigm of network marketing. When you understand this theory, you will see the importance of plugging in to the culture of achievement.

Simply put, my theory of action states that the underlying cause of all action is thought – or, more precisely, patterns of thought. We think a certain way, and then we act in accordance with that way of thinking.

Now, even though patterns of thought come before action, my theory is that these patterns often develop in order to explain or justify the required action. For example, a soldier learns to think that it is honorable to die for his cause, because on a deeper level he knows he may die, and believing such a death is honorable gives that possibility meaning.

Because most of us have been brought up in the traditional paradigm, our patterns of thinking have developed in such a way as to justify what we are expected to do in the nine-to-five world. We separate our personal and professional lives because we have to be prepared for professional disappointment. We tell ourselves we work for our family's sake, because we have to be prepared to spend a lot of time away from our family. We condition ourselves to 'live for the weekend' because the weekends are the only time that will belong to us until retirement. All of these patterns of thought lead to action consistent with what is expected of us.

Then, we switch paradigms. Suddenly, the patterns of thought that developed over the years are at odds with the actions expected of us. The obvious response, under the circumstances, is to change the patterns of thought – but that's easier said than done. To the extent that we can replace the old patterns with new ones, we can replace the old actions with new actions. And the only process proven to accomplish this is a long-term commitment to the culture of achievement.

CLUES TO THE CULTURE OF ACHIEVEMENT

To TAKE ADVANTAGE of the culture of achievement, you need some interpretative 'tools,' techniques that help unlock the value of new ideas.

1. ANALOGOUS THINKING

Analogous thinking is a powerful tool for assimilating complex processes and relating them to what you already know. An analogy takes an idea or process you're already familiar with and maps a new, unfamiliar one on top of it. This way, you can understand the new process by referring to the familiar one. In the Introduction to *Making A Difference*, I used a familiar analogy:

In 1984 I founded Nutrition For Life along with my partners Jana Mitcham and Tom Schreiter. At the time, one of our goals was to remove the physical 'failure factors' inherent in most other network marketing companies at the time. Making A Difference *is another step in that direction, only this book tackles mental and psychological failure factors, the habits of thought which can sabotage a successful new venture.*

The familiar idea is the 'failure factor' concept. To communicate the purpose of this book, I extended the analogy and referred to 'mental and psychological failure factors' (the subject of the next chapter).

2.   IMMERSION

I've already touched on the value of 'information overload.' A technical term for this phenomenon is immersion. Use *immersion* as a learning technique by taking on large chunks of new information without worrying about grasping everything. You are literally holding your head under the water as long as possible before coming up for air. This is an excellent orientation technique when you're learning something completely new. Instead of trying to capture all the data, immerse yourself in it without anxiety over missing anything, then return later for another round. The information is absorbed in stages, and the anxiety related to 'overload' is removed.

3. THOUGHT/ACTION/REACTION

Another useful learning tool is the *thought/action/reaction* exercise. When you're trying to change a pattern of thought and behavior, it helps to be able to understand how your current set of beliefs is influencing behavior. The best way to do this is to scrutinize things you 'shouldn't' do – actions and attitudes you now know are counter-productive to your success – and question the reasons for them. In this case, the action triggers the reaction, which is to search for the culprit thought. As you learn more, this exercise will also help you understand the rationale behind new patterns of action, too.

4. CORRESPONDENCES

Everything you learn is connected in some way to the larger picture. In a sense, the learning process is an attempt to make all the various pieces fit together. To do this, search for *correspondences* in training material. Correspondences are ideas and expressions that are repeated by different teachers in different contexts over time. By spotting these correspondences, you can link material in your mind and 'file' it appropriately. The more you search for and identify correspondences, the greater your understanding of the 'whole' will be.

CHAPTER FOUR

Spotting The Failure Factors

WHEN HE DROPPED HIS PEN on the floor, the unfortunate engineer bent over to retrieve it. At that moment, six more pens – the entire contents of his pocket protector – spilled onto the carpet. Undaunted, the engineer picked up three of the pens and returned them to the pocket protector. Then, he bent down to retrieve the other four. The three he'd just returned to the protector spilled out again. So, he picked up as many pens as he could – six – and put them in the pocket protector. Then, he bent down to get the last one and the six newly returned pens hit the ground again.

Something wasn't working here, and until the engineer found a new approach to retrieving his pens, he was going to have problems.

This is a humorous example, and I apologize in advance both to engineers and to advocates of the pocket protector. This is an easy example, too, in that we all immediately spot what's wrong with the poor engineer's approach. Every time he bends over, he re-creates the original problem: his pocket protector goes horizontal and its contents slide out. In real life, the failure factors are often more difficult to identify.

Before we founded Nutrition For Life, Jana Mitcham, Tom Schreiter and I had all been successful in other network marketing opportunities. In the process, we have observed a number of factors that were literally built into the programs – factors which, in our opinion, facilitated failure: front-end loading, back-end loading, breakaways, non-consumable products. One of our goals in founding our own company was to provide an opportunity that eliminated these factors.

Every industry has its own failure factors to contend with. Failure factors are built-in tendencies that lead well-meaning people to act in ways that automatically sabotage success. In network marketing, the failure factors we identified were literally incorporated into the compensation plans of the companies we were a part of; by doing the *right* thing, you actually undermined your long-term success. Jana, Tom and I discovered these factors first hand when we saw the effect they had on our own businesses.

Sometimes, failure factors are more difficult to spot. We often see the effects of a failure factor without realizing the cause. Thus, we repeat the process that caused failure and, inevitably, fail again. Like the engineer with the pocket protector, we spend our time trying to reverse the results without stopping to consider the cause.

THE BLAME GAME

IN THE LAST CHAPTER, we looked at the common "it won't work" response some skeptics have to our industry. The primary cause for this reaction is a lack of understanding coupled with a certain level of fear. A secondary cause has also been isolated: the effect of unrecognized failure factors.

Some people who have tried unsuccessfully to start a network marketing business now believe, after their own negative experience, that network marketing itself is to blame – literally, they think networking doesn't work.

Over the years, my partners and I have discovered a number of failure factors that reside, not in network marketing, but in the business psychology most people bring with them to their network marketing business. Success in any endeavor is directly related to performance, but there are some factors that can sabotage acceptable or even outstanding levels of performance. By spotting these factors in your own thinking, you can protect your business from their influence.

Taking responsibility for your own success is the first step to spotting the failure factors. It's just too easy to play the blame game, the process by which we shrug off responsibility and assign guilt to some outside source. The blame game is the common recourse of those who have not only failed at their endeavor but also given up on ever succeeding. Instead of taking a good hard look at the actions that led to their failure, they sit back in their easy chairs and take pot shots at people who haven't given up.

If you succeed as an entrepreneur, that success is due to your own initiative. Sure, you may have received support along the way, but it was your action and your action alone that caused your individual success. By the same token, if you fail, that failure is linked to your actions, too. I'm speaking from personal experience. I was an unsuccessful entrepreneur for quite a while before I became a successful one. I flirted with failure before courting success. Of course, I was tempted at the time to find someone else to blame for my setbacks, but if I had, I would never have gotten this far. Instead, I took a long hard look at what I could do to change the results I was getting – and it worked.

You see, failure is a part of everyone's life. We all fail at one time or another. After all, you can't really succeed at *everything!* The difference between people who remain failures and people who overcome failure is that overcomers use failure as a learning tool. Charlie Jones says, "How did I learn to make good decisions? By making *bad* decisions!" The same principle applies here. In many ways, failure is the schoolroom of success – but only for the student who's ready to learn.

This chapter focuses on two things: *helping you identify potential failure factors in your current thinking,* and *showing you a way to overcome them.*

WHY WE FAIL

SUCCESS DERIVES FROM ACTIONS that turn out right. The results we intended occur, and we label the result a success. Failure, on the other hand, denotes an undesired outcome. The results we were looking for didn't come through. To replace failure with success, we need to understand the way that different actions yield different results. In a sense, it's as simple as discarding actions and underlying thought patterns that lead to undesired results and replacing them with deeds and thoughts that lead to the right outcome. Of course, in practice, it's much easier to say than to do.

Applying the theory of action from the last chapter, we know that actions result from patterns of thought, and that these patterns often form in order to justify the actions that are expected of us. In other words, it's a cycle. The need for certain action dictates the development of a way of thinking, and that way of thinking leads to the desired actions. Now, if the results of those actions become undesirable (i.e., you continue to get what you've always got), then it follows that you need to change the thought patterns.

Do people really tailor their thinking to accommodate their actions? You bet they do. In fact, in some ways this process can be very detrimental; for example, when we alter our beliefs so we can 'get away' with doing things we were brought up to believe are wrong. Yes, our beliefs are fashioned by society, by our environment and culture, but anyone who denies that an individual can radically change his or her way of thinking is seriously underestimating the power we can exercise over our minds.

I noticed an example of this on a television news show not long ago. The reporter was doing a feature on Civil War re-enactors, people who dress up in blue and gray uniforms and re-create the battles of that conflict. Since my days as a history teacher, I've always been fascinated by things like this, so I decided to tune in. A few months before, I had heard an interview on National Public Radio of Tim Horwitz, author of a new book called *Confederates In The Attic*, who is a Pulitzer Prize-winning journalist for the Wall Street Journal. The book discusses the popularity of Civil War re-enactment, especially in the South, and Horwitz was featured on the news program, too.

The re-enacted battles are quite a spectacle – guns spraying blackpowder smoke, horses charging by, bugles and drums sounding. The re-enactors look like the real thing – in fact, many of them participated in the filming of the recent movie *Gettysburg*. One of the participants described what he called a 'period rush,' the exciting sense that you're actually there. It was a fascinating report.

Of course, the Civil War is not without its problems. After all, one of its main points of contention was the abolition of the pervasive evil of slavery. Anyone who dresses up in a gray uniform and salutes a Confederate flag is going to have to do some explaining, and I was perfectly prepared to hear a re-enactor explain that these activities, while they celebrate the famous battles, are in no way intended to ameliorate the horror of human slavery. Instead, I was rather shocked to hear a man explaining that slavery, after all, wasn't as bad as a lot of people made it out to be! Others insisted that states' rights, not slavery, is what the war was all about. I can't tell you how disappointing it was.

It's easy to see what had happened. I doubt that any of these people truly maintains that slavery 'wasn't so bad.' The reactions of these re-enactors, in my opinion, do not truly represent a wish to 'turn back the clock.' Instead, they had allowed their beliefs about history to alter in order to allow guilt-free enjoyment of a popular pastime. Still, it was a rather chilling example of the power we exercise over our beliefs, and how they can be made to accommodate our actions.

I'm giving you this example not to condemn Civil War re-enactment, but to show that we have to be very careful about the relationship between our thoughts and actions. Many people, perhaps without realizing it, modify their thinking in ways that allow un-ethical behavior. Think about it: have you ever seen a person who behaved unethically and later *didn't* have some justification? Of course not. Their thinking adapted before they took action, though a process they may never have been aware of. This is the 'dark side' of the subject, and I call it to your attention because I want you to understand that we are now talking about a serious subject.

In this book, I have intentionally discussed the importance of values before talking about changing unsuccessful patterns of thought. Why? Because I am a firm believer in the idea that we should change our thinking to enable us to do what we *ought* to do, not so we can get away with what we *want* to do. When people unethically manipulate their own thinking or the thinking of others, one of the first victims is the individual's natural sense of responsibility. The loss of responsibility is fatal to your hopes of success, because taking responsibility for your actions is the single most important way of insuring achievement. Without responsibility, there is no lasting reward.

THE TRADITIONAL PARADIGM'S LEGACY

IN THE TRADITIONAL PARADIGM, we have grown accustomed to two factors that combine to shape a false understanding of achievement: *salary* and *obscurity*. Now, 'salary' is a good thing (no arguments there), but it can have some undesirable effects on your thinking. You see, salary is a form of fixed compensation only occasionally adjusted to reflect performance. The average person makes the same income for productive months as for unproductive months. Of course, if you have too many unproductive months, you may lose that salary – but then again, we've become very sophisticated when it comes to manufacturing results. One of the first things you learn in the corporate world is how to look busy.

We're all familiar with the 'Peter Principle,' the idea that people in an organization are elevated to their level of incompetence. One of the circumstances contributing to this phenomenon is the fact that the person doing the elevating and the person doing the work are two separate people. You advance because a subjective evaluation is made of your work. Each time you advance, your work changes, so that your performance becomes unpredictable. Throughout the process, you are insulated from the results – positive or negative – of your performance by a little thing called *salary*.

The effect this has had on our thinking is hard to overstate. We expect to be paid regularly, and we expect the same check month in and month out. To get a raise, we can boost our performance temporarily (or appear to), and then return to a more moderate level. Salary provides fixed compensation for incremental, sometimes uneven performance. In fact, many salaried employees come to feel that they should be compensated not for their performance but for the position they hold. In other words, not for what they do, but for who they are.

In the traditional paradigm, this form of compensation has led to all sorts of unusual aberrations. Don't get me wrong: I'm not saying salary is wrong. I'm just pointing out that it's a concept which leads to certain behavior, certain expectations. And these expectations create patterns of thought that become failure factors when they are transferring into the new paradigm of network marketing.

The network marketing paradigm replaces the salary buffer with true performance-based compensation. Incredibly, it also incorporates the residual impact of a growing organization – in other words, your performance is magnified by that of your organization, so that a small increase in your performance equals a large increase in overall performance. As a model for compensation, it is far more attractive than the traditional paradigm. It is, however, *different* and therefore must be understood differently if it is to be used successfully.

The second factor I mentioned, *obscurity*, means that in the corporate world, your performance is not scrutinized consistently. Sometimes you're in the spotlight, but more often than not you are in the shade. Your compensation, even when it is based on performance, is only influenced when you are observed.

Some people have made a virtue of obscurity – they couldn't get by without it. Obscurity means doing enough to get by. It means not having to knock yourself out. It means knowing how and when to look busy without having to really stay that way. People who have adapted to obscurity have taken a megadose of failure factors. The moment they enter the network marketing paradigm, the landscape changes.

That's what most people appreciate about network marketing. Unlike the few who enjoy the illicit benefits of obscurity, most people spend their time in the corporate world trying to be noticed. They exert a lot of energy and effort hoping that someone up the ladder will notice what they're doing. Obscurity works against their advancement, because they do a good job all the time, but benefit only occasionally.

Even so, the effect of salary and obscurity creates certain failure factors in even the best people, primarily by implanting false expectations. When a person first enters the network marketing paradigm, these expectations are visible in two distinct areas. First, *they expect regular, fixed compensation immediately.* Second, *they expect consistent results from inconsistent performance.*

In my days as a distributor, I escaped these two factors. I came from an academic background and had only limited experience in the traditional paradigm. Many of my fellow distributors, however, showed signs of these failure factors early on. One man in particular always amazed me. He started out, reasonably enough, with a goal of making a certain amount of money within a certain time frame. He would say, for example, in twelve months I need to be making $10,000 a month to consider my business a success. Well, that sounded good to me. With a commitment like that, I figured this guy would be someone to watch. He came from a corporate background and I was always in awe of him – he was a 'power' networker, I suppose.

Over the next twelve months, I paid attention to what he was doing – maybe I could learn something, after all. He attended lots of meetings, he seemed to know everybody, and he was always involved in intense sessions trying to get one sideline or another going. I expected him to rocket right up to the top. He seemed to know all the right people and be at all the right places.

Unfortunately, he was building his network marketing business the same way he'd worked in the corporate world. He had lots of contacts, and hardly any downline. He spent his time 'networking' and never marketing. He explored all the angles, but stayed clear of doing the simple things that would build his business. He was measuring his success by the size of his check, but he didn't seem to be doing any of the things that would make that check grow. I was puzzled.

Needless to say, he didn't last much longer than the original twelve months. Near the end, he was the most negative person I knew. He could tell you all the problems with our opportunity, all the reasons why you couldn't make 'real' money. Out of politeness, I never mentioned to him what *I* was making – his eyes would have popped out. And the difference between us was that I focused on consistent personal performance – the hallmark of the new paradigm – and he focused on sidelines and scuttlebutt, vestiges of the old way of thinking.

To help overcome the effects of these failure factors, I suggest that you think of your network marketing business in the same way that you would a new start-up of any kind. True, your business isn't as risky as a start-up in the traditional paradigm, but many of the same dynamics are at work. In order to grow, your business will need an up-front investment of your time and effort, an investment you should not expect to re-coup right away. You must also take responsibility for what happens with your business, which means being involved in every aspect of its growth. Don't leave things to chance or assume they will take care of themselves. Get involved at the beginning and stay involved. In addition, plan on making a consistent investment of time and effort – don't build your business in spurts. Constant, consistent expansion is an essential for any growing business.

To prevail against the failure factors means wrenching your mind away from 'employee' thinking and filling it with 'entrepreneur' thinking. And that means taking profound responsibility for your actions. When you start your own business, you automatically forfeit the right to 'pass the buck.' Of course, when you take full responsibility you also reap the full, undivided benefits – another advantage to the new paradigm.

RE-LEARNING RESPONSIBILITY

Today, we use the term 'taking responsibility' as if it were synonymous with 'taking blame.' When someone admits to doing wrong, we say he 'took responsibility' for his actions. This is an unfortunate – and rather destructive – form of usage. It conceals that fact that the number one reason people do the wrong thing in the long run is that they *didn't* take responsibility in the first place!

As simple as it seems, I find that one of the areas in which we are most lacking is responsibility. For some reason, we just don't understand what responsibility means. In fact, it's a word we barely use any more, and when we do use it, it's laced with negative connotations. To overcome the mental and psychological failure factors, you've got to re-learn responsibility.

In this chapter, I've illustrated several ideas with 'negative' examples: by showing the wrong approach, we shine a light on the right one. The absence of responsibility makes itself felt in so many ways that it would be impossible to list them all. When you take action, you set events in motion. Here's an analogy I like to use. Your car has stalled and you've got to push it out of the way of traffic. You get the vehicle moving downhill, and then you have a choice: you can jump behind the wheel and guide the car, applying the brakes as needed, or you can just jog along behind it and catch up when it stops. Now, unless you have no common sense at all, you're not going to just jog behind the car. You're going to sit behind that wheel and control the direction the car is moving in. You're going to make sure you don't run into anything. You will set the car in motion and then guide it along the way.

In an example like this, the right thing is obvious. If you let the car roll without direction, you have no idea where it will end up. You have no way of controlling it. It would be completely irresponsible and you wouldn't dream of doing it – you might lose your car, after all!

Now put yourself in the parking lot of the local supermarket. You've parked a good way off, and it's a hot day. When you return and unload your groceries, you have to decide what to do with the empty shopping cart. We know that by some law of pavement design, all supermarket parking lots are built at an angle to allow abandoned shopping carts to pick up speed before slamming into a nearby vehicle. So, you have another choice to make: either you walk the empty cart through the hot sun to the nearest repository, or you do what most people do and try to balance it precariously on the pavement and make a run for it before the cart begins to move. No one would let their car roll free and unguided into a parking lot, but at one time or another we have all surrendered shopping carts to fate and hoped for the best. The difference, of course, is that we have nothing really to lose by abandoning the cart, whereas we've invested a lot of money in our vehicles.

Responsibility means staying behind the wheel when you put things in motion. It means guiding progress as things gain momentum, and even applying the brakes when necessary. Responsibility comes naturally when some valuable possession of ours is at stake. Unfortunately, we aren't always that good at determining what's at stake in the real world. Sometimes we let events take their own course, like a shopping cart rolling through a packed parking lot, never realizing that we've just placed our own self-interest at the mercy of chance. Missed opportunities, lost jobs, hoped-for promotions all roll by and we content ourselves to jog along behind them and let things take their course. It's a form of willful self-destruction we see more and more these days.

When you work for someone else, the effects of irresponsibility take their toll first on your employer and then, as a by-product, on you. Irresponsibility costs your employer money, and eventually it costs you a promotion or a raise. In a sense, the blows of irresponsibility are cushioned because they pass through the employer first. When you work for yourself, lack of responsibility – lack of involvement – take an immediate, unmediated toll on you and your business. That's why re-learning responsibility is so essential.

We've already seen that failure is one of the greatest teachers. One way to re-learn responsibility is to feel the effect of its absence. Unfortunately, it's not a very effective method. For every person who answers the wake-up call, ten hit the proverbial snooze button and repeat the same errors again and again. That's why I recommend a simple three-step process for developing responsibility among entrepreneurs:

1. KNOW WHAT YOU'RE DOING

Confusion breeds irresponsibility. If you begin with a shaky understanding of what you're doing, it will be difficult to take responsibility. You don't have to be an expert, but you should know the steps involved and how to do them. Take the trouble to learn the right way to do something before you put things in motion. Here's an example: Find out how the plan works before you show it to someone else. You don't have to be an expert, just familiarize yourself with the basic mechanics before you try to explain it to someone else.

The number one reason people wash their hands of their own projects is that they didn't really understand what they were doing in the first place. As things developed, they got out of hand and no one knew quite what to do. You can avoid this by taking the time to understand the process before you set it in motion.

2. KNOW THE BENEFIT

To monitor your actions, you need an idea of what results to expect. What is the benefit of doing this? Once you understand the benefit, you have a tool for measuring the effectiveness of the outcome. If you don't get the benefit you expected, then something was done incorrectly. Work your way through the process until you identify the failure factor.

A common error is to assume that if the benefit does not result, then the process is at fault. Never start with the assumption that the process is to blame. Today, popular business writers have laid more and more of the blame for nonperformance on flawed processes. The problem isn't people, they say, it's the process. I agree, provided the process is executed properly. Unfortunately, there's a human tendency to place blame before examining causes, and the 'process' is an easy scapegoat. Many people who are convinced the plan 'doesn't work' never actually *worked* the plan! So don't assume the process is at fault if you don't get the expected results right away – especially if you're dealing with a proven process that's worked for others. Instead, focus on how the process was executed. Look for steps which may have been overlooked, seek help from those with more experience. And above all, take responsibility for the outcome, no matter what.

3.   STAY INVOLVED

If there is one technique you can apply to solve the 'responsibility' problem, it's to stay involved. This is the most important advice I can give you. I've seen cases where people didn't really know what they were doing and weren't sure what the benefits should be, but they stayed involved and worked it out and triumphed. As long as you stay involved, you haven't failed. Failure is when you back away and wash your hands of the events you've set in motion. Involvement is a strong antidote to the failure factors.

PROVIDE YOUR OWN MOMENTUM

A RELATED FAILURE FACTOR that comes from the traditional paradigm is the reliance on other people to provide momentum. In network marketing, we see this most commonly displayed by those who begin their businesses and then wait for their upline or downline to build it for them. At its core, this approach represents one of the most damaging misunderstandings about the network marketing industry.

The main difference between the new paradigm and the old is the structure of compensation. In network marketing, compensation is tied directly to performance. You work in an environment where you can truly reach your potential. There are no limits on what you can do – no one has to vacate a position for you to move up.

Somehow the myth sprang up in the early days of the industry that the real difference between the two was that in the new paradigm, *other people did all the work.* In other words, you did your part, and then became successful when a whole lot of other people did theirs – a 'pyramid' scheme, if you will. Unscrupulous promoters took advantage of this misconception and, even today, some people come to the new paradigm with an inaccurate idea of what to expect.

If you apply common sense, you realize that the 'do nothing' approach is doomed to failure. After all, you've entered an environment where your compensation depends on performance. No performance equals no compensation, right? The more you perform, the more you can expect to earn, right? So why is it that so many people bring this failure factor with them when they enter network marketing? Simple: they don't understand *residual impact*.

RESIDUAL IMPACT

IN NETWORK MARKETING, you earn commissions on sales throughout your organization. As your organization grows, you earn higher percentages of more volume. Obviously that's an incentive to build an organization. Another incentive is the *residual impact* of your business building efforts.

A few years ago, the city of Houston built a tollway not far from Nutrition For Life's World Headquarters. It's a very convenient location for us: you can get on the tollway not far from our office and head straight to the George Bush Intercontinental Airport. When we go on business trips, we all take the tollway to the airport. Like most tollways, ours allows you to purchase a sensor for your car that automatically debits your account when you pass through the toll-booth. It's a lot more convenient than scrambling for change and waiting in line – especially if you're late for your flight! Everyone loves the tollway, because it's so convenient. When it was finally completed, the city actually threw a party up on the highway, with a band and everything. It was quite a spectacle.

Construction was completed on the tollway a couple of years ago, and ever since we've had to pay whenever we use it. Even once the original construction loans are paid off, the tollway will continue to collect our money. We don't really mind, of course, because of the convenience. It's a win-win situation. In essence, the work that was completed several years ago is earning a profit today, and will continue to earn one into the future. The work has a tangible residual impact in the community, and that translates into tangible *residual income* for the investors.

In network marketing, a similar dynamic is at work. As it grows, your organization acquires a momentum of its own. This momentum is made up of hundreds or even thousands of people in your organization who are trying to expand their own businesses. As they build their organization, yours grows, too, creating an exponential growth factor. And this in turn creates *leverage*. Now, your actions are being multiplied and magnified beyond your own ability – you derive benefits that are actually multiples of your own performance. In theory, you could stop building your business and it would continue without you.

And that's why some people think their businesses are going to be built by someone else: they forget that for an organization to gain momentum, *you've got to build it first!* Although network marketing is a better way to benefit from your performance, it's not a license to stop performing – far from it. Considering how much more beneficial the new paradigm is, if anything, it's an encouragement to do more.

The residual impact of network marketing involves a number of complex factors, more than we can touch on here. The important thing to remember is that action is the catalyst for residual growth. A residual is, by definition, an echo of expended energy. Before you get the residual, you've got to expend the energy.

A REALISTIC TIMEFRAME

"How LONG DO I HAVE to build my business before I get residual income?" A question I hear all the time. My standard answer is, "Plan on working from two to five years to build a solid business." Sometimes I feel bad about giving that answer – it doesn't always take that long – and sometimes I doubt that the person asking will ever see residual growth. Why? Because of attitude. When you start talking about timeframes, you inevitably introduce what I call the 'walk away' contingency. In essence, you're saying, "How long do I work this before I walk away?" That's dangerous thinking.

When you start a new business, any kind of business, your commitment should be total. Time limits and exit strategies can act as subconscious release valves, sending your mind the message that it's all right to give less than 100%. When I hear someone say, "I'm going to give my business six months to get off the ground," I am amazed. What kind of commitment is backing that business up?

Time frames and conceptions of 'realistic' waiting periods are major failure factors. I say waiting periods rather than working periods because in my experience, people who set time limits intend to wait it out rather than work it out. Whatever you do, don't put a time limit on your business!

Of course, there's nothing wrong with setting time-related goals. In fact, the added pressure of a time-sensitive goal can be very inspiring. Sometimes we do our best job under that kind of pressure. Each year at Nutrition For Life's Annual Convention, our leaders often make commitments to reach the next level of achievement by the next convention. People in the audience promise themselves they'll make it on stage next year.

That's what happened to Dr. Tom Klesmit. Dr. Tom had been in Nutrition For Life for just six months when he attended his first Annual Convention. He was so impressed by what he saw that he promised himself he'd be up on stage the following year. Well, he outdid himself. Not only was he on stage, but he was honored as one of the top three achievers in the entire organization! That's a powerful endorsement for setting time-limits on your goals and sticking to them.

The thing to remember, however, is that no one has any idea how long your business needs to reach maturity. We can estimate time periods based on the averages, but each business is unique. The only way to find out how long your business needs to reach a level of momentum and create residual impact is to build it.

HOW TO HANDLE FAILURE FACTORS

WE'VE TOUCHED ON several major failure factors that people carry with them from the traditional paradigm when they enter network marketing. More importantly, we've laid some groundwork for overcoming them. Now, I want to share some useful techniques for handling failure factors you encounter while building your business.

1. SQUARE PEG, ROUND HOLE

The most important thing to remember is, don't try to make something fit if it doesn't. You may have a high level of expertise in the traditional paradigm, and many of those skills will serve you well in network marketing. But be aware that others won't. When you find a skill or technique just isn't working in the new paradigm, don't blame network marketing – discard the technique. Also, be open to learning new ideas and skills that were designed with networking in mind.

2. DON'T RE-INVENT THE WHEEL

After more than five decades, the patterns for successful behavior in network marketing are fairly established. It's human nature to want to add our own flair to everything, but make sure you learn the basics first. Here's a common conversation in our industry – *New distributor:* "I just thought of this great idea! It'll put me way ahead of everybody else!" *Sponsor:* "Yes, some people tried that in the early 80s, but it didn't turn out to be as effective as they hoped." The lesson? Don't re-invent the wheel!

3. WORK THE PLAN, NOT THE ANGLES

Perhaps the most important general rule for avoiding unexpected failure factors is to focus on the simple business building system and stay away from sidelines and 'new' angles. You came to network marketing to build a business, not to get bogged down in side ventures and alternative schemes. Yes, it's tempting to look for alternative 'revenue streams,' but the time you spend chasing these things would be much better spent invested in your core business. Once you've made a commitment to building a network marketing business, that commitment should be total. Any side activity has the potential to draw away your focus – and your growing business can suffer.

CHAPTER FIVE
Putting Yourself In Charge

IN HIS EXCELLENT BOOK *Leading Change*, James O'Toole points out that: "People in groups form fixed ideas, and all of the forces within the group conspire to protect those notions, no matter how outmoded or inaccurate they may be." Overcoming the fixed ideas of the traditional business paradigm has proven to be a difficult task. O'Toole demonstrates that for over forty years, the attempts of experts like J. Edwards Deming and Peter Drucker to replace these notions were simply ignored by the mainstream. Trying to change the traditional paradigm from within is a slow, torturous process.

In the first four chapters of *Making A Difference*, we have looked at some of the most pervasive 'fixed ideas' of the traditional business paradigm. We've also provided strategies for breaking free from these fixed ideas and replacing them with more effective ways of thinking. In the last chapter particularly, we saw how important it is to take responsibility for your own success.

Now, we're ready to proceed to the next level.

Who do you work for? It's a simple question, but it rarely gets a simple answer. "Well, I work for my boss, for my spouse, my kids, the mortgage company, sometimes my friends – and that's just for starters." Critics are fond of pointing out how selfish this generation is, how focused it is on its own needs and desires. The 'me' generation is shrugging off its responsibilities, turning its back on its obligations, and seeking out short-term – and often self-destructive – satisfaction. Maybe so, but in that case, why are so many people so *aware* of all the different people and institutions they're 'working' for? Why are they sacrificing their time and effort to contribute to someone else's gain? It doesn't sound like selfishness to me.

Most people I talk to are very sensitive to their obligations, to the point of being over-burdened with them. Meeting the needs of so many other people can have a debilitating effect. But what can you do? Your spouse needs you, your kids need you, the bills have to be paid, your friends and family expect certain things from you – the list goes on and on. You can't just ignore all these needs, so you do the best you can, you spread yourself as thin as you can, trying to please everyone.

But that can only last for so long. Your motivation level slackens, your energy drains, and soon you're simply going through the motions. After a while, you get to the point where you just don't *care* anymore. And that's when you rebel against all the obligations and shrug off all the duties life has imposed. The phenomenon so many critics have labeled as 'selfishness' is really the effect of a well-meaning but misguided selflessness that has simply been pushed too far.

At the root of the problem is the fact that we don't work for ourselves. We subordinate our own desires to the needs of others. We force ourselves to be content with benefiting only second-hand from our actions. We donate our time and energy to other causes in return for various forms of compensation which usually have one thing in common: they aren't what we really want. What we *really* want we relegate to the realm of dreams, to the land of a happy retirement that may never happen. *One day*, we'll live for ourselves, but *today*, we live for others.

In Chapter Two I insisted on the importance of focusing on others rather than yourself *within the context of relationships*. In a relationship, that's the right thing to do. But when it comes to your work and – more importantly – the motives for your work, there's only one answer and that's to put yourself in charge.

REACHING ONCE

ONE OF THE CHALLENGES we face as parents is knowing where to draw the line between what we do for our children and what we expect them to do for themselves. Much of our time is spent equipping our kids with the skills to do things on their own. We teach them to tie their own shoes, and there comes a point in the process where we refuse to do it for them. Why? To develop character and independence. We want our children to learn that the best way to get help is to help yourself.

If you raise an only child, these lessons are largely academic, but when you have a number of children, each one competing for your attention, it becomes very important for your kids to learn to help one another and to help themselves. After all, as good as your intentions are, you can't ignore one child to see to the needs of another – at least not for long. As the youngest boy in a big family, I learned this lesson the hard way!

No matter how pure and noble our intention to help may be, our energy and attention is divided. We can only offer rare moments of concentration before our other obligations are neglected. The more directions you reach out in, the shorter your reach becomes. To reach the farthest, you have to reach once and never pull back.

Perhaps the ultimate paradox of achievement is that *the only way to meet your many obligations is to put your own needs first.*

I frequently travel by air, and it has always amazed me that one of the most important lessons of success has been drilled into me over and over again by flight attendants during the safety demonstration. The next time you're on an airplane, pay attention to what they have to say. If, in the unlikely event of an emergency, the air masks drop down from the overhead compartment, your instructions are to first attach your own mask, and only then to see to the needs of others. I wonder how many times a parent travelling with child has heard that instruction and winced. How could you worry about putting your own mask on when your child is sitting beside you without one? It seems heartless. But it's the right thing to do. Once your need is met, you are free to assist your child with your full attention, without anxiety, and consequently you will do it faster and more effectively.

The reason so many people who spread themselves so thin to help others simply can't sustain it is they haven't put on their mask first. They're struggling to insure a supply of oxygen to others and they aren't getting enough air themselves. Learning to breath properly is so essential when you undertake any kind of activity – when I ran track in college it was probably the most important skill I learned. If you're getting enough air yourself, you can sustain your actions over a much longer period of time, without the fatigue. The same is true in life. Ironically, many of us conduct our lives like untrained athletes – literally holding our breath in anticipation and robbing ourselves of the strength to stay the course.

If you want to run the race ahead of you – if you want to win – you must focus on one thing. Too many of us try to do it all. We try to compensate for every weakness instead of developing a single, monumental strength. The higher truth of achievement is that running your own race well is the only way to help others run theirs. Right now, the best thing you can do for the people you love is drop them from your list of 'bosses' and put your own name there instead.

Without a successful business of your own, you lack the wherewithal to fulfill your obligations. If you work to pay off a debt, you'll never see the light at the end of the tunnel. If, on the other hand, you work to achieve lasting success, you can make good on all your debts as a by-product. The best way to meet expectation of others is to surpass them pursuing a greater goal of your own.

INFLUENCE AND POWER

WHEN IT COMES to getting things done, we usually distinguish between two separate means: influence and power. Power is your ability to dictate how a thing will be done, or your ability to do it yourself. Influence is your ability, in the absence of power, to have something done the way you want. Influence and power both have to be earned. Clearly power is preferable because its results are easier to predict and control, but business authors tend to emphasize the role of influence, because it is easier to obtain and can often be just as effective. To compensate for its lack of 'force,' influence is more difficult to lose and abuse.

Power is generally divided into two types: *positional power* and *personal power*. As the name suggests, positional power is derived from the position you occupy. An office manager wields positional power within his or her organization, just as a monarch, to a much greater degree, wields positional power within a kingdom. There are good managers and bad managers, just as there are good and bad kings and queens, but their power is not enhanced or curtailed by whether they are good or bad – it simply came with the job.

Personal power is a slightly misleading term. A better one, although not as alliterative, would be 'compelling influence.' In other words, personal power is a measure of your ability to compel people you don't officially command to do things your way. Two major sources of personal power are extreme charisma and strong relationships. Although we can't always control how charismatic we are, we've already seen how strong relationships are built. If you know how to build strong relationships – and you do – you have the ability to cultivate personal power.

Some authors draw a moral distinction between personal and positional power, implying that personal power is somehow better than positional power. They draw this conclusion after observing how frequently positional power is abused. Unfortunately, personal power can be abused just as easily. When we talk about power, we have to realize that power can be used to do good things and bad things. Within a framework of values, power works for useful, positive ends. Without that framework, power is as unpredictable as an abandoned shopping cart in the parking lot – only much more devastating. As we discuss taking charge of your circumstances, I cannot emphasize too much the importance of developing and exercising power within the context of the Core Values.

The goal of every enterprise is to get something done. All things are accomplished through the application of influence and power. Some things are more difficult to accomplish than others, and we tend to rate the size of the ambition by how much influence and power are required to accomplish them. Paying your bills, for example, is considered to be a more modest ambition than, say, ending world hunger, because the former requires dedication and personal discipline while the latter demands a volume of power and influence which none of us possess or can aspire to.

To reach your goal, you must build your power and influence. The amount of power and influence you need depends on the size of your goal, but the methods of achieving it are largely the same. Personal power and influence, for example, are cultivated through strong relationships and charismatic leadership. Positional power is acquired by rising in an existing organization or founding an organization of your own. Combined, influence, personal power, and positional power provide the means of making a difference in people's lives.

Let's look at some specific ways of developing power and influence in network marketing:

1. INFLUENCE

Influence is the easiest of the three to obtain, because it is based on the example you set for others to see. People are influenced by those they admire or aspire to emulate. Literally, we listen to people whose success we want to duplicate. When you listen to a presentation by a leading distributor in your organization, even if you don't know this person personally, you are influenced by the example they set. You listen to what they have to say and you apply it. Even though you have no relationship with this person, and they have no power over you, you willingly hear them out. That's influence. Of course, you don't *have* to do what they say, but the odds are you will consider it.

If you want to influence other people, begin by setting an example that others can aspire to and respect. That's the first step. The second step is to communicate your message the right way.

Now, the best way to learn to communicate that message is to read Dale Carnegie's classic *How To Win Friends And Influence People* – perhaps the greatest book ever written on the subject. In a nutshell, you have to communicate ideas in a way that people can make them their own. You've seen people suggest an idea in such a way that the man they're talking to thinks it was his own idea. That's an example of effective influence.

2. PERSONAL POWER

The most common form of leadership in network marketing is leading through relationships, which is the exercise of personal power. Before you can lead in this way, you must build the relationships.

In every relationship, there are times when you act as leader. By the same token, there are also times when you defer to the leadership of others. In a reciprocal relationship, this shifting balance of power is natural and healthy. Power in the context of relationships is not an exercise of command; instead, it's an expression of shared self-interest. The leader uses power to benefit both parties.

Since we have already covered relationships at length, let's say a few words about leadership by virtue of a charismatic personality.

Sometimes it's easy to focus on the negative side of charisma – the Hitlers and the Stalins – rather than looking at the far more common examples of ethical charismatic leadership. Like power within relationships, power derived from charisma is subject to the willing participation of those who are led. In other words, it is a form of reciprocal relationship even when no personal relationship exists between the leader and follower. And, it's a very emotional relationship, which accounts for the fact that we either love or hate charismatic leaders, not for their message but for their *personality*.

Most forms of power are cultivated for a higher cause. Charismatic personal power is the exception, as it tends to develop as a part of a person's personality whether he or she aspires to it or not. As a result, many charismatic leaders find that they have a following before they have a message – a curious dilemma! This is one of the things that gets them in trouble, because people want rock-solid consistency out of their leaders, and this is sometimes difficult to have when your concern is primarily with *being* a leader, not with leading people to act in a particular way.

That's why charismatic leaders more than anyone else need the framework provided by the Core Values, to give their project substance and a firm foundation. When charismatic personal power is used in a deserving cause, it is one of the most powerful and inspirational agents of change known to man. In fact, I would go so far as to say that *all* great achievements need some form of charismatic personal power to be accomplished.

Developing charisma is not an easy process – in fact, many experts agree that you either have it or you don't. I disagree. You see, at the heart of all charismatic personal power is a radiating belief level. The thing all charismatic leaders have in common is that they inspire belief in others. In fact, their power derives a large part from the belief they pass on to their followers. In a sense, charisma is telling people what they want to hear and *believing it*.

3. POSITIONAL POWER

When you have positional power, people listen to you because you're the boss. When it's tempered with personal power, positional power is the most effective way to get things done. It cuts through every objection and sets aside every obstacle. Properly used, positional power is a major force for positive change.

Does positional power exist in network marketing? Interestingly enough, it does – but in a wholly unique form. Each distributor in the organization has a position. The value of that position is determined entirely by how it is built. Every position is equal at the beginning – a ground-floor start-up, so to speak – but as the entrepreneur commits more time and effort into building the business, certain positions emerge as points of leadership.

Positional power in network marketing is really a form of personal power, but it is based on the strength of the position the distributor holds in the organization. Stronger positions merit more respect and authority. You gain positional power by building your own network marketing business. Through personal achievement you embody the old Roman idea of *primus inter pares* – first among equals.

After all, in our industry, you promote yourself. Positional power in the traditional paradigm is usually something that others bestow upon you. Here, you give it to yourself by building an organization of your own.

BE YOUR OWN BOSS

THE PHRASE 'be your own boss' jumps out at you from the classified ads of every local newspaper. Today, opportunities are a hot commodity. More and more people want to get out from under their nine-to-five job and call their own shots. They want to put themselves in charge.

I became a network marketing distributor because I wanted put myself in charge. Later, I was invited to join the management team of the company I was involved with. I had some misgivings –

after all, I'd be working for somebody again – but I saw it as an opportunity to help correct some of the failure factors I'd already begun to observe in the company. So, I divided my time between home and my new office at the company's corporate headquarters in Dallas. I held a number of positions there – head of distributor relations and head of marketing, to name a couple. It was my first real taste of corporate life – even though I was working, ironically, for a *network marketing* company.

Every day, I worked with people who were building their businesses. I always felt I had something special to offer because I had done the same thing. Now, I was making a difference in people's lives by sharing my own experiences and helping to make the path smoother for those who came after me. I had strong relationships with many of the distributors I'd worked with in the field, and now I also had positional power in the corporate sense – people were working for me on behalf of the distributors I represented. I was like a missionary, advocating the needs of new distributors at all the corporate meetings, helping to produce new tools and new support procedures. I really felt good about what I was doing, and I was committed to the company in a major way.

Interestingly enough, our headquarters was located in a shiny golden skyscraper, one of the buildings featured in the opening credits of the hit TV series *Dallas*. Every time I saw the program, I could make out where the window to my own office was. "David," I said to myself, "now you've *really* made it."

Unfortunately, I was about to learn a lesson that would stay with me for the rest of my career.

The owners of this company were people I looked up to, people I had trusted as a distributor and who were trusted by thousands of other distributors. When you spend your time and effort building a network marketing business, the one thing you have to be able to rely on is that the company providing the opportunity will be there for you. That company has to be solid and committed for the long-term. Much to my surprise, this one wasn't.

In the early years of network marketing, instability was a major problem. Like any fledgling industry, ours was struggling to find its feet. In the process, many company management teams were put to the ultimate test and only a handful survived. Every company – in our industry and in the traditional paradigm – goes through a testing process, a phase of uncertainty. These periods test the commitment of management and distributors alike. Today, with the support of more experienced companies and organizations like the Direct Selling Association, it is easier for new companies to stay on course.

When I realized that the company I had made a lifetime commitment to was going to shut its doors, I felt sick. I couldn't believe it. This went against everything I knew to be right – I had never even considered that *quitting* was an option. It was a terrible blow to all of the distributors, and I was one of the people who stayed on as long as possible trying to help sort out the mess the owners had left behind.

You can spend a lifetime cultivating skill at leadership and success, and without commitment and integrity you've achieved nothing. I made two promises to myself after that experience: First, that I would start a network marketing company of my own, run according to sound principles, and second, that no matter what happened I would stay committed to that company. When people entrusted their legacy to me, I would not let them down.

My partners Jana Mitcham and Tom Schreiter shared that resolve. They, too, had seen what could happen when commitment is lacking. When we founded Nutrition For Life, it was a company not only determined to make a difference but *committed* to make a difference. We would stop at nothing less.

If you're going to be your own boss, then it's up to you to make a commitment. People often make the mistake of thinking that skill or special ability determines success. They don't. When you put yourself in charge and take responsibility for your own success, the only thing that matters is your commitment. How focused are you willing to be? How many obstacles are you willing to overcome? How many short-cuts will you pass by to stick to the right path? Those are the most important questions you can ask yourself. Do you have the staying power? Are you in this for the long term? Are you building a dream or just daydreaming? If you're serious, if you make a real commitment to taking charge, you will make a living *and* a difference – guaranteed.

FIVE STEPS TO BEING IN CHARGE

IN THE TRADITIONAL PARADIGM, business suffers from a profound lack of leadership. Management training programs rake in millions of dollars each year preparing candidates for positions in an ideal world, leaving them totally unprepared for what's waiting for them in the workplace. When positional power is used ineffectively, relationships suffer, influence and respect drain away. All because we are never taught how to be in charge.

It's not so difficult, but it requires a new mindset. Here are five steps that I've found are extremely effective when you're in charge of your success:

1. PUT YOUR FUTURE FIRST

Every decision you make should advance your fundamental goal. If you find yourself doing things that don't move you forward, you're probably putting other considerations ahead of your own future. The only way to meet your obligations is to focus on your strengths and let the rest take care of itself. As difficult as that can be, it is essential.

Imagine all the different commitments and obligations you have right now. How many of them will you still have six months or a year from now? Probably all of them. Now, how many of them would you be in a better position to deal with if you were more successful? Probably all of them. If you concentrate on your own success, you will be better able to fulfill your commitments and obligations. If you don't, then a year from now you will be in the same situation you are in today.

2. BELIEVE

Your belief level draws people to you. Without belief, plans fall apart. People lose focus and drift away. When you take responsibility for your success, you also take on the role of encourager – inspiring others with your own unshakable belief. As we've noted, a high level of belief boosts your charisma and results in profound personal power. Like commitment, belief is a strong catalyst for action.

3. SET THE RIGHT EXAMPLE

You're a leader now – so act like one. To gain the respect of others, you must do the things you expect others to do. The people you lead will accept your expectations only if they see that you meet and exceed them yourself. Also, don't worry about what other people think. Align yourself with the Core Values to insure proper orientation. As others, through your influence, do likewise, they will come to see the value of your example. The worst thing you can do as a leader is to compromise on principle. If people don't see something different about you, they won't feel the need to discover something new about themselves.

4. MAKE STRONG RELATIONSHIPS

You can't do it alone. You need the support of strong, committed lieutenants. The only way to get this support is to build other people through relationships. Cooperative, win-win enterprises are led by men and women who invest heavily in relationship-building. When you're in charge, you must develop a new respect for the autonomy and individuality of other people. You need them as much as they need you – make sure they know that.

5. PROMOTE YOURSELF

Your success is in your hands. Nothing stands between you and the top of this industry but time and energy. By building your business, you literally pull yourself up through the organization. This is a vital point: you have started your own network marketing business. You work for yourself, setting your own goals and making your own plans. You have successfully entered the new paradigm. Even if you're only building your business part-time, you have an incredible opportunity to take advantage of. The trail to success has already been blazed. The necessary steps have already been identified. All that remains is for you to duplicate the system. As you do, you build a position in an organization all your own – and you make a difference in the lives of real people every day.

CHAPTER SIX
The Duplication Principle

THE INVENTION OF THE PRINTING PRESS in the fifteenth century sparked one of the most profound, if unacknowledged, revolutions in the history of mankind. In scope and significance it resembled nothing so much as the digital revolution we are living through today. Within the space of a generation, the entire intellectual landscape was transformed. Rare books and manuscripts that had been in danger of destruction were suddenly available in abundance. Generations of learning and knowledge, so far reserved for the elite, were now accessible to scholars throughout the land. The printing press sparked a rebirth of the culture at large – indeed, *the* rebirth, the Renaissance – all because a man named Gutenburg had solved the problem of duplication.

Gutenburg didn't invent duplication. For centuries, scribes and copyists had duplicated rare manuscripts. Some centers of learning maintained armies of scribes churning out volume after volume. To accomplish their task, the copyists developed techniques that helped them improve their memories and insure the accuracy of their texts. They became highly prized specialists with years of training. An elaborate system was in place to duplicate books in the Middle Ages, and at the time it seemed effective. But men like Gutenburg were not satisfied – they saw the problems with this form of duplication.

First of all, copying a book by hand was a complex process. To participate, a person needed a high level of skill and aptitude, along with years of apprenticeship and training. For one thing, scribes had to be able to read and write, and that eliminated well over 95% of the population! Even in the hands of veteran copyists, the work took a long time, and it was very expensive. The resulting product was beyond the reach of all but the wealthiest of clients. In addition, there was no such thing as an exact duplicate. Each scribe had his own style, worked with his own illustrators, and added his own gloss on the text. Because of all the specialized skill that went into the process, it was only natural that each book became a unique work of art. Sometimes the artistry of the copying was placed before the accuracy of the text. So, although the process worked, there was undoubtedly room for improvement.

The printing press revolutionized the duplication process by creating something that had never existed before: uniformity. Now, a scholar in Paris and a scholar in Nuremberg could study an exact copy of the text, a copy that was identical page for page. The duplication process was faster and produced more – the average printing run, even in the late fifteenth century, was between five hundred and a thousand volumes. For the first time in history, people all over the world could be literally 'on the same page.'

Every revolution draws its strength from duplication. Ideas and beliefs are spread from one mind to many, with the result that people act together and work for a common goal. To the rest of society, this common purpose is truly revolutionary. It goes against the grain of the usual cycle of compromise and mediocrity. Suddenly, institutions we thought would never fall are gone, and prejudices we thought we'd never escape are overcome. In a revolution, we learn to live beyond our personal limits, to take part in something larger than ourselves, to leave our comfort zone and never look back.

In the excitement that surrounds a revolution, we often overlook the simple mechanisms that make the whole thing possible. The fifteenth-century printing revolution was that way. Elizabeth Eisenstein, in her book *The Printing Revolution in Early Modern Europe*, calls it an "unacknowledged" revolution. The role of the printing revolution in the Renaissance is all but forgotten. In the same way, many of the tracts and treatises that fueled the American Revolution have faded from memory. A generation from now, the computer will be such a facet of people's lives that they will forget the breakthroughs and innovations that made it all possible. The causes of a revolution may be remembered, but the *means* of revolution are often overlooked and forgotten.

In this chapter, we will examine the underlying cause of a revolution that is transforming business culture just as radically as the digital revolution is transforming communication: the network marketing revolution. At the heart of this movement is a concept so simple, so reasonable, that it is often overlooked. Alone, your personal strengths and limitations mark the boundaries of your success. If you understand and apply the principle of duplication, you can go far beyond these boundaries and create a personal revolution all your own.

WHAT IS DUPLICATION?

If the printing revolution began with a new way of duplicating texts, the network marketing revolution was sparked by a new way of duplicating action. To understand duplication, you need to grasp the process itself and the context it happens within.

Duplication is as simple as it sounds: it consists of copying or replicating the successful actions of another person. It is an age-old principle that finds a unique expression in our industry. Ten workers harvesting a field accomplish more than a single farmer. They can work faster and cover more ground. In the same way, ten achievers working together grow faster and expand across more territory than a single entrepreneur. By building an organization that duplicates your actions, you magnify your own effectiveness exponentially.

We are all familiar with common forms of duplication. Common sense tells us that the smartest way to build a business is to find out what works for other people and copy it. In networking, this occurs within an organization. Each member of the organization is building a business, and in the process is adopting ideas and techniques from other networkers, trying to figure out what works best.

Duplication is a by-product of every organization, but duplication alone is not enough to insure success. After all, the process of duplication is content-neutral. Bad, ineffective techniques can be transmitted with just as much ease as good, effective ones. Without the proper management, duplication can spread the wrong ideas instead of the right ones. Your goal as you build your organization is not just to create duplication, but to create *successful* duplication.

Unfortunately, *successful* duplication is not so simple. It is human nature to adopt successful ideas, but it is also human nature to *adapt* them. Instead of building on the achievement of others, we have an alarming tendency to tear them down. You've heard the expression, "Don't re-invent the wheel"? The odds are, when the first wheel was made, rather than building carts, the other people gathered around to criticize the new invention and explain how *they* would have done it. That's human nature. We would rather sit in our armchairs and devise hypotheses than replicate effective techniques developed by someone else. For some reason, we seem to be willing to trade the benefits of precise duplication for the questionable distinction of having devised our own unique approach. You can imagine the early inventor standing next to his square wheel saying, "It doesn't work – but it's mine!"

STUFFING ENVELOPES

ONE OF THE MOST BENEFICIAL TASKS I've ever undertaken was stuffing envelopes. I learned more about success from stuffing envelopes than almost anything else I've ever done. Most people don't like to stuff envelopes. When there's a mailing to go out, it's amazing how many people vanish. They think stuffing envelopes is a boring, methodical task with no redeeming virtues. Nothing could be further from the truth.

The first thing you learn when you're stuffing envelopes is that the more people you have, the faster the work is done. In a sense, you have to build a temporary organization to get the mailing done. You recruit whoever passes by – you don't pre-judge your prospects! – and you show them what to do. Each addition to the organization increases your productivity exponentially.

The second thing you learn is that there is an effective system. When you start, each individual arranges his or her material and chooses an order to stuff things in. As the work progresses, people start looking around to see whose sequence is working best. Then, everyone adopts the most effective system. Every individual in the organization has his or her papers arranged the same and replicates the same work-flow. When new people join the group, they aren't left on their own – the more experienced members show them the system and even arrange their materials for them.

The third thing you learn is that someone on the outside always comes along to criticize what you're doing. Usually, this person is unwilling to help, although he offers his opinions and advice quite freely. The members of the group who are focused on the task pay him very little attention.

The fourth thing you learn is that there's no room for innovation. This is the toughest lesson. In every group, there's always someone who thinks he has a better way of doing it. Unlike the critical outsider, he's a member of the group, and his intentions are good. He isn't happy just repeating the actions. He wants to be recognized for some new addition to the method, some new technique or idea that improves things. In essence, he wants to be personally responsible for the success of the group, even though the group is already successfully accomplishing its task. In practice, this member ends up wasting a lot of time re-arranging the materials, making unnecessary suggestions, testing alternative sequences. Not only is he not contributing to the success of others, but he's actually diminishing it by decreasing his productivity and distracting others.

The fifth and final lesson you learn is to focus on the benefits, not the process. If we could get the benefits we want from a single action, there would be no problem. No one argues over how to stuff a single envelope. The difficulty comes from the fact that, to get the desired benefits, we have to commit to a sequence of actions repeated over time. Time is the critical factor. Anything can happen over time. We get distracted over time. We lose focus over time. Over time, we begin to doubt. The key to success is to focus on the benefits and let the process take care of itself.

I've seen some interesting things happen while people stuff envelopes. They begin to talk, to share stories, even to sing. They're thoughts are elsewhere, but their hands repeat the action steps. They are motivated, part of the team, and they're even reluctant to leave the group. When the work is finally done, I've seen them stick around and talk more, not ready to lose that sense of camaraderie. What a strange phenomenon! What an *instructive* phenomenon! If that sense of community can keep people focused while stuffing envelopes, imagine what it could do to keep them focused while they build their dreams!

The five lessons I've ascribed to stuffing envelopes have obvious application to the art of effective duplication. Let's take a look at them again.

1. THE MORE PEOPLE YOU HAVE, THE FASTER THE WORK IS DONE.

Before you can duplicate, there has to be an organization. The power of duplication is unleashed through people, through relationships. You cannot tap into that power alone. By the same token, duplication has a transforming power that can make an impact on literally anyone. The best argument against pre-judging prospects is that, through duplication, anyone can achieve success. Every member of your organization makes a valuable contribution in his or her own right, no matter what skills and knowledge they bring to the table.

2. THERE IS AN EFFECTIVE SYSTEM.

We aren't traveling uncharted territory. Success in network marketing can be – and has been – achieved. The pioneering days are over and there now exists an effective system of actions to be duplicated. The workflow has already been established, so all you have to do is participate.

3. SOMEONE ON THE OUTSIDE ALWAYS COMES ALONG TO CRITICIZE WHAT YOU'RE DOING.

Naysayers appear in every business, and focused team members don't give them much notice. No great deed was ever accomplished without criticism. The press ridiculed Abraham Lincoln, and George Washington was actually burned in effigy! If these great men could not escape attack, no one can. By the same token, Washington and Lincoln did not allow the criticism of others to blunt their purpose. If anything, the attacks strengthened their resolve. They had the integrity and character to convert the criticism of others into fuel for their dreams. We should all strive toward that example.

4. THERE'S NO ROOM FOR INNOVATION.

Once an effective system is established, the need for core innovation is gone. That doesn't mean the system is set in stone. Systems do change over time, but the impetus for change is refinement through action, not innovation. In other words, the system improves because it is better understood and applied, not because it is replaced. The actions themselves should be the focus of your energy, not the desire to 'improve' them. It's only natural for a novice with an incomplete understanding to think he sees a 'hole' in the existing method. My advice is this: always question your understanding before you question the system. You will save yourself a lot of time and effort, and you will avoid prolonging the benefits of your actions.

5. FOCUS ON THE BENEFITS, NOT THE PROCESS.

What do you do with your dreams and your goals while you repeat the action sequence? This is a vital question, because the leading cause of failure is lack of belief, not doing the wrong thing. To do 'the right things long enough consistently,' you've got to have the proper mindset. Otherwise, your belief levels sinks and you descend into a rut. I always say, "Knowing the reason prevents the rut." When you connect with the benefits, you keep the process fresh and alive.

CONCEPTS, TECHNIQUES & STRATEGIES

ALTHOUGH IT SEEMS like there are many different ways to learn, there is really a single pattern that seems to apply in every situation. Our knowledge and understanding grow in three distinct stages. We grasp *concepts*, then we master *techniques*, and then we comprehend *strategies*. A book like this, for example, is primarily concerned with concepts – the 'big ideas' that underlie successful network marketing. A typical training session teaches techniques, the specific actions that spring from the concepts. Later, when you achieve success and recognition, you begin to see strategies, the larger patterns that spring from the momentum the concepts and techniques create. Only when you reach the level of strategy do you begin the path to true mastery.

In network marketing, the substance of duplication is technique. The things you duplicate are effective techniques, actions that consistently provide certain outcomes. For example, there is no 'perfect' way to recruit new members into your organization. There is, however, an extremely effective method to show the plan, one that seems to work more than any other in a wide variety of circumstances. In Nutrition For Life, that technique is as simple as showing prospects a specially-designed presentation on video. It's simple, effective, and easy to duplicate.

If the substance of duplication is technique, then its context is conceptual. The techniques work in any context, but they only make sense to those who understand the fundamental concepts of network marketing, the ideas this book was written to communicate. Now, a person with no idea of the context can certainly apply the techniques and succeed – but a person with understanding finds it easier to do. When you understand the concepts, you find yourself better equipped both to duplicate the techniques and to model them for others to follow.

When I coached high school athletes this three-stage process was obvious. We never taught players the fancy moves. We never talked about complex strategy. We just focused on the fundamentals, the simple techniques every player had to master. In basketball, we taught boys how to dribble, how to shoot, and how to pass. We taught them how to play their positions. Every player had different strengths, but they all had the same repertoire of techniques. If some players outshone the rest, it wasn't because they knew techniques the others didn't, it was because they had a greater conceptual understanding of the game.

When we say someone is 're-inventing the wheel' what we're really saying is this person is trying to modify the techniques. I experienced the same thing coaching basketball. Everyone wanted to have a fancy dribble, a signature shot, a special technique that none of the others had. As coaches, we tried our best to eliminate this attitude. For every fancy move that worked under stress, there were ten that ended up with the ball bouncing off someone's foot or hitting the side of someone's head or dropping into the hands of the other team. These would-be innovators cost us more points than their signature moves ever won.

Star achievers aren't born on the technical level. They reach their full potential on the conceptual level. They have a greater understanding of the game, and it adds something almost intangible to the way they apply the techniques. They have an edge not because they know other, secret techniques, but because they understand the simple basics better than anyone else. They know the 'why' as well as the 'what.' To achieve mastery, your focus must be the same. Learn the techniques and practice them. When it comes time to move beyond the basics, don't try to come up with new techniques. Instead, go back to the concepts and learn a deeper understanding of the basics.

What about strategy? Strategy is illusive. So many books have been written about strategy that you would expect it to be a simple thing to learn. Nothing could be further from the truth. In fact, even the terms are wrong. Strategy isn't something you *learn*, it's something you *earn*.

A common mistake novices make is to try to practice strategy rather than technique. Instead of showing the plan, they spend their time *discussing* it with other distributors. Instead of applying simple techniques, they put action on hold and do 'research.' They always want more information before they will act. In essence, they won't do *anything* until they understand *everything* – not a very realistic outlook, but a surprisingly common one. The irony is that only by applying technique consistently over time will you begin to understand strategy.

Many people have a conceptual understanding of network marketing but no practical experience applying techniques. Others have applied certain techniques without an understanding of the foundational concepts. You can have concept without technique and technique without concept. But you can't have strategy without both concept and technique. To reach the higher level of proficiency – to begin the journey to true mastery – you have to know the ideas and practice the skills.

This point was driven home for me quite recently. When you do as much traveling as I do, it takes a toll on your luggage. A few months ago, I visited a new luggage store and bought a new set of matching suitcases. It was an impulse purchase. I hadn't planned on buying anything, and when the first young salesman approached I told him I was just looking. He nodded and went back to a conversation he'd been having with another salesman. When I spotted the luggage I wanted and decided to make a purchase, he was still talking. I looked around for someone to help, and a young woman in her mid-twenties came along. She was new to the store but very helpful, offering all kinds of information about the luggage and even giving me discount credit for a sale that wasn't scheduled to start until the following week. I left the store with so much luggage I was afraid it wouldn't fit in the car!

Several months passed, and I dropped in on the same store. One of my suitcases had been damaged by the airline, and I wanted to see if I could get a replacement. When I walked in, I spotted the young woman who had helped me before, but I didn't see the two salesmen who'd been having a conversation while I shopped. To my surprise, the young woman recognized me and asked how my luggage was doing. When I told her about the damage to the case, I expected her to say there was nothing they could do. Instead, she said, "That suitcase should have held up better. Bring it in and we will repair it at no charge." I was amazed – she had not only remembered me from all those months ago, but she was still concerned about my satisfaction, even so long after the sale. I ended up buying some more pieces, and in the process she revealed that the day I had bought the luggage from her, my purchase had pushed her over the sales quota and she got to go home early. "The guys weren't too happy about that," she said. "The one who talked to you first thought he should have gotten credit for the sale!"

"He was talking to one of the other salespeople!" I said.

Although he hadn't done the work, he'd expected the benefit because he'd gone through the motions when I first walked in. Not surprisingly, the young woman I was talking to turned out to be the top salesperson at the store, and both of the men who'd been talking instead of working had long since left.

I thought about this on the drive home and it really brought home a lesson. When I was young, I worked in retail stores, and I know how strong the temptation is to talk about the job instead of doing it. Anyone who's ever worked in a retail store knows the type of salespeople who spend most of the time chatting and complaining, but who consider themselves to be experts, somehow superior to the ones who are actually helping customers make their purchases. They think they understand the job, and they expect all the benefits, but they don't apply the simple techniques that get the job done. As a result, they never get ahead, whether they work for someone else or they work on their own. They want to start out at the top, and they excuse themselves from putting out real effort until they get there.

Fortunately, there is another type, the one that lets the big picture take care of itself and just does the job. Ultimately, these are the people who advance, because they're the ones with a true understanding of the process. Life tends to be pretty fair in its promotion policy – it only advances the people who pay the price.

CAN YOU DUPLICATE IT?

Have you ever followed another driver when you didn't know the directions to your destination? You rely on the other person to make sure you can follow. You expect them to brake at yellow lights so you don't get left behind. You expect them to signal their turns in advance, so you can follow. You expect them to drive at a moderate pace rather than leaving you back in the dust. If a driver follows these rules conscientiously, you can follow him or her anywhere.

If you want your organization to duplicate your actions, make sure they can follow you. Make sure you're taking a path everyone can walk, and signal your moves in advance. Duplication is a natural process – it happens no matter what. If it's possible, your organization will duplicate your actions. So the two questions you have to ask yourself are: 1) *Does it work?* and 2) *Can it be duplicated?*

For better or worse, people will duplicate your actions. If what you're doing doesn't work for you, it won't work for them, either. By modeling ineffective or unproven techniques, you undermine your entire organization. To better understand this distinction, let's look at the principle outside network marketing. Let's say you were going to buy a retail franchise. Common sense would dictate that you'd invest in a franchise that was doing well at other locations, something that had been tested and proven, something that was making money for other business owners. Now, suppose the people selling you the franchise had never actually started a retail store and managed it? Suppose they had devised what they believed would be a successful franchise – from scratch, as it were – and sold you one. No one else had ever done it, no one knew if it would work or not. How confident would you be in a franchise like that? You wouldn't have any confidence at all!

Now, suppose the same thing were to happen in your network marketing business. You sign up and then discover that your sponsor, who is also just starting out, has devised an entire plan of action from scratch, based on what he thinks might work. It has never been tested, but your sponsor, who has never built a business before, thinks it should work. How confident would you be under these circumstances? Don't ask.

When we reverse the roles and you are the sponsor, do you want to be modeling unproven techniques to your organization? Do you want them to do what you think might work, or what you *know* will work? The answer is obvious: you want your people to be successful and that means modeling techniques that work. In other words, you have to promote the proven business-building system.

We will discuss the dynamics of this system in more detail in the next chapter. For now, you need to understand that the value of a system is that it has been proven to be effective by other people. It answers the first question of duplication. Does it work? Yes!

The second question – can it be duplicated? – is just as important. Not long ago, one of Nutrition For Life's Platinum Executives shared the story of how he had changed his approach to building the business. His background was in sales, and when he first started the business he drew on that background extensively. He brought every technique he'd ever learned to bear on his prospects and used all his sales know-how to move product and bring people into the business. Then he made a shocking discovery: none of his new distributors had his sales skills. "I had a choice to make," he said. "Either I did all the work for them, or I changed what *I* was doing so they could do it, too." He had asked the question, "Can it be duplicated?" and the answer was an emphatic "No!" So, he changed his approach. "Now," he said, "I just show the video – anyone can do that!"

The question of duplication is especially pertinent in the context of sponsoring, because people won't join your organization if they see it requires skills they don't have. If your method of building the business is beyond their scope, they can't duplicate it. A number of experts have pointed out that the fundamental question a prospect asks about any opportunity is, "Can I do this?" A major advantage of promoting an easily duplicated system is that prospects see that they *can* do it.

LEAD BY EXAMPLE (OR NOT AT ALL)

THE ONLY WAY to lead in network marketing is by example. The greatest leaders this industry has ever seen are the ones who have the courage and determination to build their own organizations in a way that can be duplicated by others. Sometimes, that does require courage. Many leaders are people of extraordinary ability, people with a much wider array of techniques and abilities than the average achiever. They could build their business any way they wanted. The reason they build it using a simple, easily duplicated system is that they want others to be able to build it, too.

The moment you sponsor other people into your organization, you become a leader. Your example, for better or worse, will be duplicated by your new distributors. If what you say and what you do are in conflict, they will follow what you do, not what you say. Think of it this way: people know that to get the results you're getting, they have to do the things you're doing. Now, if everyone in your organization is getting the results you are getting, what will that mean for you? If the answer is "nothing," then you aren't doing the right things. Strive to maintain a level of action that, if it were duplicated throughout your organization, would help move your business to the next level. If your level of action, duplicated throughout the organization, would result in the status quo being maintained, then it's time to take inventory of your actions. If you aren't getting the results you'd like to see others getting, then find someone who is and start duplicating what *they're* doing!

In the traditional business paradigm, we have grown accustomed to double standards where personal examples are concerned. We no longer expect managers to live up to the standards they set for their subordinates. Promotion means greater privilege and greater responsibility, but in the traditional paradigm, the former is invoked much more often than the latter. The rules for the boss are different than the rules for everyone else. That's an attitude many people are trying to escape when they come to network marketing. They are ready for a change. They are ready to do whatever it takes, with one proviso: they aren't going to do it alone. Whatever they see you doing, that's what they signed up for. If the example you set communicates the wrong expectations, it isn't your prospect's fault.

One of the first things that happens to people when they come to network marketing is that they become much more aware of the personal example they set. First, they are aware of it in terms of their personal requirements, the things they have to do to get their own business up and running. Then, they begin to see the influence their example has on other people. Over time, the relationship between personal example and organizational performance becomes quite clear. Is the leader motivated because her organization is thriving, or is the organization thriving because the leader is motivated? All we know is that the two are inseparable.

TAPPING INTO THE POWER OF DUPLICATION

THE CONCEPT OF DUPLICATION is not difficult to grasp. The power of duplication is not difficult to appreciate. When you do the right things long enough consistently, you make a statement. When you and your organization do the right things long enough consistently, you start a chain reaction. The impact of everything you do is magnified through duplication.

Duplication supercharges some organizations and devastates others. It supercharges the groups where proven techniques are modeled, and devastates those where pet theories and inaction rule. Either way, duplication will have an impact on your organization. It's up to you to determine what that impact will be.

Here are a few ideas to help you take advantage of the power of duplication:

1. SET THE RIGHT EXAMPLE

I cannot repeat this too many times. Duplication is like a powerful rocket, and your example provides the coordinates. If you are doing the right things on a personal level, your organization will get the right directions to follow. If not, don't expect them to succeed in spite of you.

2. MAKE SURE PEOPLE CAN SEE IT

The value of your example depends on whether or not people can see it. Make yourself visible in your organization by attending meetings and training, working with individuals to help schedule meetings and show the plan, and achieving recognition by your upline and your company.

3. USE THE TOOLS

Most companies and large organizations provide support tools that help train you and your people. These tools help you set the right example and help others to follow it whether they are in your direct circle of influence or not. In Nutrition For Life, we provide a monthly training program, a market-wide network of events and functions, and a complete line of business-building tools and support options. These tools help foster the culture of achievement – the perfect environment for effective duplication to occur.

RETURN TO THE CONCEPTS

DUPLICATION IS ABOUT technique, and after a while you will develop a full repertoire of effective techniques. When you feel you need to improve your execution of techniques, get back to the fundamental concepts and review the foundations of the business. *Making A*

Difference emphasizes these fundamentals – when you reach that point in your business, it will be time to re-read this book. Be sure you understand the relationship between the concepts and techniques. The conceptual framework exists to help you understand and apply the techniques – without action, the concepts are meaningless.

CHAPTER SEVEN
It Takes A System

IF COMMITMENT AND HARD WORK were enough, we would all be successful. Unfortunately, it takes more than that. For years experts have groped in the dark trying to quantify the personality traits and sure-fire belief systems that make successful people successful. The answers are as varied as the books, tapes and training courses that proliferate the market today. What does it take to be successful? Everyone has an opinion, and in a sense everyone is right. If you examine the personal level, you will find all sorts of traits that could be considered characteristics of success. The problem is, the personal level is not where success is born. It doesn't take skill or ability or timing or good luck to be successful. Plenty of people with some or all of these things have missed the mark. It doesn't take any particular personal trait or knowledge to be successful. What it takes is a system.

Have you ever noticed that people who are successful at games of 'chance' never ascribe their success to timing or know-how or natural ability. Instead, they admit, "I've got a system." They say they've *learned* to be successful by taking advantage of an informed series or sequence of actions. In some cases, they developed their own system, in others they learned it from someone else. The thing the systems have in common is that they're based on principles *outside* the individual. They work – *when* they work – because they're based on true principles, not because the individual is 'lucky.'

Even so, most people today are basing their success in life on mere chance. They don't have a systematic approach to achievement. Instead, they do whatever comes to mind in sporadic bursts, hoping for the best, never grounded on true principles and never certain what the outcome will be. When their projects come to naught, they are quick to blame others – or even 'fate.' The things they manage to accomplish lack staying power and rarely stand the test of time. And they simply can't understand why they always fail when other people no smarter or more talented than they are succeed!

Every task known to man must be accomplished systematically. This is obvious when we look at physical tasks such as building a house or manufacturing a car. We accept that these things are too complex to be undertaken haphazardly. They require knowledge and expertise. No one would dream of beginning work on such a project without a precise system in place to get the job done.

When we move to the abstract realm of business achievement, all that common sense disappears. Physical complexity is both easier to appreciate and less daunting than the abstract challenges of achievement. We accept that a mechanical device requires a system to be built, but never realize that a business needs the same methodical approach. We would never stand at an automobile assembly line and "wait for something to happen," but that's exactly what we do in business. The thing that sets successful people apart from the rest is that they understand the need for a system in order to build.

Successful people think more in terms of 'systems' than their peers. They know instinctively that things are accomplished through a process, and they spend time discovering or developing a process before committing their resources. In fact, in network marketing, a good way to judge the business maturity of a prospect is to see what he or she is most interested in knowing. If a person seems most interested in knowing the details of the business building system, you can be fairly sure that he or she is a success-oriented achiever.

THE SYSTEMATIC IMPULSE

THE MOST EXCITING ASPECT of the learning experience is that moment of serendipity when a new piece of information suddenly clicks into an existing framework. We call these "Aha! Moments" because they have all the power of a new discovery. If you stop and think about it, most of your education consisted of learning various systems of knowledge. When some new piece of information comes your way, and it fits into one of these systems, you find yourself thinking, "So *that's* where it goes!" You've made a new discovery, uncovered a new relationship between two seemingly different sets of information.

To be of any use, knowledge must be systematized. New data has to be catalogued and assigned a place in our overall framework of information. We generally discard what we don't understand, or we build a new framework to accommodate it. As we get older, it seems to get more and more difficult to build these new frameworks. Suddenly, we find ourselves at odds with all this new information, rejecting it. This is usually considered to be the result of a generational gap or simply old age, but the reality is it is a failure to build new systems to accommodate new information.

When you make the transition from the traditional business paradigm to network marketing, you have to make room for a new framework. You're going to be receiving some new information, and before you can make heads or tails of it you'll need a place to put it. You'll need to start a new system. Later, the connections will snap into place and you'll experience those "Aha! Moments" as you relate the new knowledge to what you already know. But if you don't start by opening your mind to the new framework, you will find yourself discarding and even rejecting some valuable knowledge.

So far, we've talked about the organization of information, but let's not forget about the organization and systemization of *action*. That's what's really important in the context of achievement. Where are you going to store the new techniques you find in network marketing? How are you going to see the relationships between these new actions and what you've done before? All of these discoveries will be made within the context of a system.

EFFECTIVE SYSTEMS

LIKE DUPLICATION, systems spring up whether you plan them or not. In the 'stuffing envelopes' analogy in Chapter Six, we saw that during the course of the work an effective system emerged. Soon, everyone adopted the system in order to increase his or her productivity. In general, *a system is any workflow pattern or sequence of actions that leads to consistent results for a variety of people over a period of time.* To better understand the system that exists for building network marketing businesses, let's take a look at four unique components of any system:

1. SEQUENCE OF ACTIONS

At the heart of any system is a sequence of actions that have been proven to be effective. The system exists to organize these actions properly and put them in the right order. It also serves as a framework for teaching the actions to others. When a workflow is systematized, it can be easily transmitted and duplicated by others. By its very nature, a system is designed to encourage duplication.

2. CONSISTENT RESULTS

The system's value derives from its ability to generate consistent results. That's why we distinguish between a 'system' and an 'effective system.' Not all systems are created equal. To be effective, the system has to repeatedly provide reliable, steady results. In other words, it has to *work*.

3. A VARIETY OF PEOPLE

There is a difference between a *personal* system and an *effective* system. To be effective, a system has to work for a wide variety of people. In other words, it cannot derive its strength from the skills or abilities of a particular individual. A talented person can make a flawed system work, but the same system in the hands of someone else will fail. Most workflows break down at this point – they worked fine for the person who invented them, but not for the world at large. They were based on the unique assets of a single person, so they don't work for other people with different skills and needs. To be worthwhile a system must work for everyone.

4. OVER TIME (DURATION)

A successful methodology must stand the test of time. In other words, it must work today and tomorrow and ten years from now. As long as the sequence of actions is being repeated, the system must produce results. That means it has to be based on principles and technologies that will last. It also means the system should be adaptable, taking advantage of opportunities to grow as times change. On the other hand, changing times should never render the system – or even parts of it – obsolete.

THE FOUR FACTORS ABOVE assume one thing: that you make a serious commitment of time and effort. No system will work if you ignore its workflow or pursue it half-heartedly. Many people refer to their company or their system as a 'vehicle' – a good example of analogous thinking. Unfortunately, some of them are thinking of a car, where you turn the key and let the engine take care of the rest. This analogy is a crippling way to relate to your business. Yes, it is a vehicle, but think of it as a bicycle. Its energy comes not from some unseen engine but from the effort you put into it. Admittedly, the mechanism is designed so that with a little effort, you see major results. And you can put enough energy into the vehicle to achieve momentum. But the vehicle is simply a tool for channeling power you yourself contribute. If you think of your system that way, you will see that the results you achieve will be in direct proportion to the commitment you make. This realization will change your whole outlook on achievement!

HOW SYSTEMS DEVELOP

EVERY SYSTEM DEVELOPS over time. One of the great fallacies is the belief that a system can be manufactured from scratch. I should know. My company, Nutrition For Life, was one of the first in the industry to introduce a complete, company-integrated business-building system. It was a complex, sophisticated turn-key system that covered every aspect of a person's network marketing business. At the time, there was literally nothing like it in the industry. Yes, there were other systems, and we had drawn on their successes to model our own, but this was a system that outpaced them all in sheer capacity and potential. Even now, I look on its development as one of our proudest achievements.

Even so, in the long run, that system was not effective. It had all the ingredients. It met all four of the standards discussed earlier. In fact, it was a model for others to follow. According to every standard of measurement known to us at the time, it should have been phenomenally successful. But, alas, it wasn't.

You see, there was one factor no one had anticipated that made all the difference. We had assumed that you could take all the best from all the different systems and synthesize it into one ultimate package. In a sense, we were perfecting generations of wisdom and know-how in a kind of network marketing laboratory. And, like most things developed in the laboratory, it could never quite bond with the outside world. Technically, it was exceptional, but it was conceived in a test-tube, not in the field.

Our company's top distributors – leaders like Dayle Maloney and Dale Brunner – went a long way to making the new approach work. Of course, they have proven over the years that they can make *anything* work! But the fact remained that to be truly effective, a network marketing system has to develop in the field.

At that time Nutrition For Life had all its ducks in a row. We were financially secure, we had an innovative product line, and we had over a decade of successful management experience. The one piece in the puzzle we needed was a true field-developed business building system, one that could match our company-designed system for sophistication and effectiveness but had the added power of being born not in the 'laboratory' but in the real world.

In 1995, it began to develop. The most important factor in the new and improved system's development was that it was tested and perfected by distributors in the field. Tools were developed and perfected with input from the people using them. New insights helped fuel the development process. Many of the techniques and principles of the previous system remained in the new one, and many more were refined and perfected. The partnership between the company and its distributors began to create a unique, effective system that produced consistent results.

Four years later, that system has developed into a comprehensive, easy-to-duplicate model for the industry to follow. It combines generations of network marketing know-how with new discoveries from the cutting edge of marketing. Most importantly, it meets the four criteria we looked at earlier *and* it was tested and proven in the real world by people who built lasting, successful businesses with it.

Explaining the nuances of this system is beyond the scope of this book, but we will take a little time to understand its significance and what it means for a new distributor joining Nutrition For Life.

If you are new to network marketing, or if you have not yet decided to build a network marketing business, then there are five things you should know about the Nutrition For Life system. I am not trying to 'sell' this system – the results speak for themselves. Rather, I want to provide information that will help you put this system in context and evaluate it in light of what you already know about this industry.

1. THE SYSTEM DEVELOPED ORGANICALLY

The first thing you should know is that this system grew over time and went through a number of development stages. Some features were expanded while others were removed. Through experience and testing it was perfected. Performance was measured. Yes, the system was engineered and master-planned, but it was also allowed to grow naturally and take a shape all its own. Results shaped and informed the underlying theory to produce a completely unique action sequence and workflow.

2. THE SYSTEM PUTS DUPLICATION FIRST

One of the reasons this system is so effective is that it is so *simple*. We all have a tendency to make things more complicated than they need to be. We make things harder than they really are – and that inhibits duplication. Throughout the development of this system, the ability to duplicate the workflow has been paramount. That meant simplicity and ease of use above all else. Let's look at an example: showing the plan. In the earlier system, we had developed a complex, highly specialized way of showing the plan, a method that took all the various psychological factors into consideration. The result? You had to be an expert to show the plan! Not anymore. Today, showing the plan is as simple as pushing the 'play' button on the VCR. As we've already seen, anyone can duplicate it.

3. THE SYSTEM STRIVED FOR MAXIMUM EFFECTIVENESS

Over the past four years, a number of different tools have been developed and tested. In time, each tool was refined and improved, always with the goal of achieving maximum effectiveness. It wasn't enough for something to work – it had to work *better*. This is an important point to grasp. Many of the tools available today have been revised and expanded since their first introduction to make them more powerful. Rather than simply producing *new* tools, the existing ones were perfected. This attention to maximum effectiveness makes the Nutrition For Life distributor's tool arsenal one of the most powerful and focused available today.

4. THE SYSTEM WAS TESTED

Perfection is achieved through testing and revision, not inspiration. When it comes to building a truly effective system, 'genius' is useful but long, hard work is the key. Nutrition For Life's system is the product of years of testing and revision, infused with moments of brilliant inspiration. The distributors of Nutrition For Life have truly paid the price to build and perfect this system, and its remarkable effectiveness is a tribute to their persistence and dedication. This system belongs to them.

5. THE SYSTEM GETS RESULTS

That says it all, doesn't it? Using this system, people build strong, stable network marketing businesses. They achieve significant part-time income. They achieve real residual income. Over time, with effort, they make their dreams come true. People of every sort find success through duplicating this system. This is the ultimate measure of any system's effectiveness.

I HAVE SHARED THESE five points for a reason: when you start your network marketing business, these five things mean that you can have *confidence* in the business building system. You can make a commitment to your business in the knowledge that the workflow you're duplicating leads to the results you expect. You can dedicate yourself 100% to working the plan, because you know you can rely on your company, your organization, and – above all – your system.

THE SYSTEM, DUPLICATION,
AND THE CULTURE OF ACHIEVEMENT

BY NOW, you should begin to notice some overlapping relationships between the duplication principle, the system, and the overall culture of achievement. The tools and events that help to create the culture of achievement are part of the system, and the system's goal is to facilitate the duplication of effective techniques. These three things support one another. They help nourish and maintain one another. In fact, to benefit from any one of them, all three must be in place.

The ideas we're about to cover are some of the most complex thoughts this book has touched on so far. Don't expect to grasp everything at once. It takes time to absorb this information. Soon, you will come to understand all this and more. For now, try to spot the new information and relate it to what you already know.

The object of duplication is to duplicate the system. Each member of an organization should duplicate the system in his or her own business. The purpose of the culture of achievement is to communicate the system – to teach it, explain it, and support it over time. The culture of achievement also facilitates duplication by bringing certain messages direct to each participant – avoiding the 'filtering' effect that happens when information passes through too many hands. Without the system, duplication is ineffective. Without the culture of achievement, the system lacks power. Without the system and duplication, the culture of achievement is impossible to attain. All three exist in relationship to one another, each equally essential.

In Chapter Three, we introduced a concept called "Thought/Action/Reaction." This is the best way to understand the relationship between the culture of achievement, the system, and duplication. Each process has a particular sphere of influence. The culture of achievement focuses on the life of the mind – on thought. The system, of course, organizes action. And duplication is the process of creating an appropriate 'reaction' throughout the organization. Together, they create a whole new environment for doing business.

Duplication is a conduit, a communication channel, and the system is the message that channel communicates. The culture of achievement creates the context where this communication is possible. What this means in practical terms is that, to create duplication in your organization, your distributors must be 'plugged in' to the culture. For that to happen, you must be personally practicing the system. So it all goes back to the all-important question of your personal example.

Success is achieved not personally but systematically. Even so, your personal actions have a dramatic impact on your own success and that of others. We've already discussed why your personal example is so critical – it provides a blueprint for duplication. So if we take what we've learned so far about the relationship between the system, duplication and the culture of achievement, we can work out two personal imperatives:

1. <u>YOU</u> HAVE TO WORK THE SYSTEM

You know your organization will duplicate your actions, not your 'message.' You can expect them to follow the system to the exact degree that you do, no more. Don't expect the person you sponsor to be more committed than you are. Don't expect the person you sponsor to do more than you do. The most important thing you can do personally to create success in your organization is to work the system in its entirety.

2.   <u>YOU</u> HAVE TO PLUG INTO THE CULTURE

First of all, you can't work the system without participating in the culture of achievement. It's impossible. That means you've got to read the books, listen to the tapes, attend the events and functions, strive for recognition, edify your mentors, your upline, the company. Second, you can't transmit the system to others by personal example alone. The culture of achievement exists to do what you cannot: to immerse each member of your organization in the training, the motivational environment, and the information flow necessary to achieve and maintain success.

ON A PERSONAL LEVEL, the fundamental question remains the same: if what you are doing personally were to be duplicated throughout your organization, would the results be worth the effort? If you are following the system and participating fully in the culture, then the results of duplication will strike like lightning! If not, then all the effort to create duplication has been wasted.

At this point, it becomes obvious that personal commitment is still the catalyst for achievement.

MASTERING THE SYSTEM

The system is a set of effective techniques. These are the precise techniques required to build a network marketing business, perfected over time through extensive testing and measured results. Everything you need to build a business is contained within the system, and the system consists of a finite number of techniques. Therefore, you can gain a working knowledge of the system through practice and study – you can learn it and make it your own. At the same time, there's a difference between learning the system and mastering it.

I know a number of people who have mastered aspects of the system. I know many people who are on the path to mastery. No one has 'mastered' the system. In the sense that the system continues to reveal new depths to all of us, no one ever will finish mastering it. The path to mastery lacks a final destination, but makes up for the lack by offering the most exciting journey possible.

Right now, it is too soon for you to think in terms of mastering the system. You should be focused on grasping the concepts, applying the techniques and making the necessary connections. You don't have to master the system to build a successful business. In fact, one of the beauties of an effective system is that it works whether you fathom it or not. You don't need to understand the system at this point – you need to *work* it. The time for mastery may come, but it is not so much a goal you seek as a goal that seeks you out.

In the early days of Nutrition For Life, our office shared a storefront with a printing company and a karate school. Each afternoon, a pack of young students would arrive – each wearing the white karate *gi* – for instruction. You could measure each student's level of achievement by the color of the belt – white, yellow, red, or black. Although I've never studied the martial arts, I do know a little bit about the process from having observed it next door.

Beginners learn how to do simple actions like kicking or punching. They also do exercises designed to condition their bodies, to get them ready for the more complex techniques. They do a lot of stretching and 'toughening' exercises. The goal of the beginner is to get his or her basic form down, to learn the stances and movements properly. It's the same way with any physical endeavor. Your body isn't used to doing things this way, so you work on the fundamentals over and over again. If you venture further before you've made these fundamentals part of your style, everything you do later will be weakened. The repetition and the drills are designed to re-train your body to a new set of actions, to make those actions automatic.

As karate students progress, they learn more complex sequences of actions called *kata*. In a way, these sequences are like complex dances. They combine all the basic kicks and punches and movements in a certain order, so that by learning the *kata* the student learns how to do all the basic actions on the move. The more advanced the student, the more complex the routines become.

The actions themselves are important, and if you learn to do them effectively they work. But the actions alone are not the full story. In the martial arts, practitioners are divided into 'external' and 'internal' artists. The external artist has the movements down but doesn't draw his energy from the deeper psychological level. The mechanical content of his routine may be perfect, but the emotional content is lacking. The internal artist, by contrast, draws on a deep well of internal power to execute his actions. On the outside, it may look like the two are performing the same moves, but the trained eye sees that the internal artist brings a much deeper level of mastery to the actions.

When we speak of mastering the system, we're talking about the same thing. On the surface, two achievers may appear to be doing the same action, but one brings a radically deeper level of mastery to it. Rather than duplicating the technique externally, he reproduces it from an internal source of power that creates a whole new dimension to the exchange. The two achievers may use the same words and apply the same techniques, but the one who draws on the inner source experiences more power and effectiveness.

So the question is, how do you achieve this kind of inner power? How do you acquire this deeper level of mastery? The answer is similar to the one you find in the martial arts. Many people think that a point comes in the student's training where the teacher pulls him or her aside and shares the 'secrets' of mastery. The student has one of those "Aha! Moments" and his art is transformed. Well, that's not how it happens at all. Remember, the appearance of the actions – both internal and external – are often the same. The new content is often invisible to an outsider. No secret additions have been made to the technique. Rather, a new understanding has come about. No doubt the new understanding is partially due to the influence of a mentor, but *the real determining factor is not the sharing of secrets but the conscientious consistent practice of the fundamentals over time.*

In other words, the path to mastery consists of doing the basics long enough and consistently enough to come to a new understanding of them. Mentors and masters can help in this process, but it is mainly a personal discovery. As we've already seen, it is something that cannot be learned – it has to be *earned*. Here are some tips to help you find the path to mastery:

1. PERFECT THE DETAILS

Most students don't want to wait. They look at the basics as something to get out of the way so they can proceed to the more advanced lessons. As a result, they often learn the technique without perfecting the details. They move on too quickly and never discover all the nuances of even the simplest techniques. The power of most actions lies in the details, and if you perfect the details, you begin to master the technique. In fact, you don't need many techniques in your arsenal if you take the time to master each one.

2. ASK QUESTIONS / EVALUATE ANSWERS

Be careful about making assumptions about why something works. The most important learning tool you have is the ability to ask questions and evaluate answers. Sometimes you learn not from receiving one right answer but from getting ten wrong ones. Always question the techniques you use, always ask yourself and others why they were effective and how they could be more effective. Always ask if you could have applied the technique more effectively. Carefully weigh the answers you receive and see if you can find some new insight into the action. This is a powerful way to gain knowledge.

3. PRACTICE TECHNIQUES FROM EVERY ANGLE

A simple technique, perfectly understood, can be used in a variety of situations. You can adapt it in infinite ways. To take full advantage of what you learn, you should practice each technique from every possible angle. Try a particular type of invitation on a number of different people. Use a particular audiotape with a variety of prospects. Even if you aren't able to put these techniques into immediate use, practice them on your own or with another distributor. Work on your presentation and delivery. Perfect your techniques and adapt them to new environments and situations.

4. LISTEN TO YOUR CRITICS

Two sets of people whose criticism you should always take to heart are your knowledgeable mentors and your prospects. Your mentors know what they're talking about. They've been through the situations you're in right now – they've seen the technique you just blew work perfectly somewhere else. Listen to what they have to say and apply the advice they give. Even if it doesn't make sense, give it a try. You may find you've been approaching things from the wrong point of view. Also, listen to your prospects, whether they decide to join or not. The feedback you get from them can be invaluable in adjusting your actions.

5. READ THE BOOKS

Immersing yourself in the literature of achievement is essential to reaching the path to mastery. Books play a unique role in the development of a leader. They are the ultimate classroom and the lessons they teach are not available anywhere else. They fill your mind with fresh insight. When you spend time with a book, you absorb the author's perspective and learn to see things differently. You have the opportunity to evaluate your progress from someone else's point of view. More importantly, books fuel the inner artist – they turn your gaze inward and lead to a deeper appreciation of what you already understand. I recommend that you adopt a disciplined regimen and read at least one new book every four weeks. In addition to achievement literature, you should also be reading classic fiction, prose, and poetry. There are many paths to mastery, and opening your mind through books is one of the most effective.

6. STRIVE FOR RECOGNITION

The quest for mastery is most beneficial when driven by a genuine desire to achieve recognition. When we talk about recognition, we mean acknowledgment for achievement, not attention for its own sake. You see, the criteria for recognition in most network marketing opportunities – certainly in Nutrition For Life – correspond to levels of personal and professional development. In striving for recognition, you strive for real achievement.

CONSISTENCY

THE MOST IMPORTANT ADVICE I can share about the quest for mastery is something my father taught me. He never discussed it with me. Instead, he made his life a model of one essential principle: consistency. My father was a baker. Each morning he got up while the rest of us were asleep and went to work. He baked things fresh each day – it was a point of honor. He lived each day for its own sake and faced them all with an impressive consistency. He didn't deviate from his purpose, and he didn't try to do *more* than a day's work. Each day he did precisely what the day demanded and kept the rest until tomorrow. He didn't plan for rainy days because he didn't believe in them.

The principle of consistency has hunted me down throughout my life. My father's influence in this one area has been so strong that I couldn't escape it if I tried. After seeing my dad give his best each and every day, I would be ashamed to do any less. He left behind a powerful legacy without ever saying a word about it. In his own way, my dad achieved mastery of his walk in life. Ever since, I have wanted to follow him in my own walk.

Emerson wrote that "a foolish consistency is the hobgoblin of little minds," and as a result *wise* consistency has gotten a bad rap. Consistency compensates for every shortcoming. Consistency divides life into manageable portions. Consistency lets you do your best without reference to yesterday or tomorrow. Consistency keeps you in the moment when other minds are wandering. Consistency is the most powerful tool for mastery I have ever uncovered, and I recommend it to you highly.

Some people believe that great deeds are accomplished by great gestures, that sudden dramatic all-or-nothing risks are what changes the world. Nothing could be further than the truth. The real power behind change is modest, consistent action taken over time. All the bakers in my hometown working together and giving their all for one glorious day couldn't outdo what my dad did on his own throughout a lifetime. His little bit, performed consistently over time added up to the most inspiring example in my life.

Success in network marketing isn't about quitting your nine-to-five job. It's about quitting your nine-to-five thinking. You can set aside a portion of your time and consistently build a network marketing business that will provide you with a realistic income and an opportunity to go beyond and achieve financial freedom. That's what the business building system is all about. That's what duplication and the culture of achievement are designed to support. You can make modest, realistic investments of time and energy on a consistent basis and achieve a return that the traditional business paradigm simply isn't designed to give. That's the remarkable truth about network marketing. It doesn't require any special skill or ability, and you don't need any unique personal traits, either. Success comes from a system you can work consistently and persistently over time to achieve results.

By this point in the book, we have touched on the essential framework for understanding network marketing. We've seen the importance of leaving traditional thinking behind, of immersing yourself in a new perspective with a new set of principles and a unique collection of proven techniques. Our discussion of the business building system brings all these new ideas together into a single, coherent, radically different paradigm. In the chapters ahead, we will see how this new information sheds exciting new light on the age-old question of making a difference and making a living.

CHAPTER EIGHT
Building People

THE NETWORK MARKETING INDUSTRY is famous for drawing circles. Sometimes it seems like we can't explain *anything* without drawing a few circles! The circles represent people in an organization, they illustrate the relationships between sponsors and distributors, upline and downline. The circles are invaluable as a tool for communicating how the plan works and how organizations are structured. The circles can also be misleading.

Your organization isn't built from circles. It's made up of people.

People are unpredictable. They don't act according to any pre-determined rules. You cannot predict what people will do, and you certainly can't *control* them. People do not 'fall into line' and they certainly don't organize themselves like neat little circles on paper. Although you can work to understand people, you will probably never reach that lofty goal. After all, we sometimes have trouble even understanding ourselves.

And yet, for all their unpredictability, your business *relies* on people. You not only need people, but you need them to do their best. You need the members of your organization to perform, to build their own organizations, to reach their own dreams. You need them to be committed, motivated and ready for action. It's a tall order, and the success of your business depends on it.

So, what do you do? How do you build a stable and solid business from building blocks so unpredictable as people? Well, *before you can build a business, you've got to start building people.*

WHAT DRIVES YOU?

HAVE YOU EVER ASKED yourself what drives you to do the things you do? Why do you make the commitments you make? Why do you participate in the groups you belong to? Many people think that they act according to their beliefs – that they do what they do because of what they believe. The problem with this argument is, we believe in a lot of things we don't do anything about! We sympathize with good causes without joining them. We agree with noble truths without spreading them. We applaud daring initiatives without taking the stage ourselves. This is only natural: we are passionate about more things than we can possibly do. The question is: what makes us commit to the thing we decide to do?

If you want to understand other people, begin by examining yourself. Like all of us, you have limited resources, and you've made decisions about where to invest your time and energy. Again like most of us, you realize there are other things you might have done: by making the choices you have, you've had to sacrifice other things. We all do. That is the nature of commitment.

When you introduce other people to your organization, you are asking them to make a commitment. That means making a sacrifice, too. People who willingly make that sacrifice will remain committed. Those who make the commitment without coming to terms with the sacrifice will have doubts later on. When you choose to do something, by default you are choosing *not* to do other things. Sometimes the lure of other things can be tempting. That's why it's important that people who join your organization do so for the right reasons, with the proper understanding of the commitment they are making.

But first, you have to make a commitment of your own. And a sacrifice.

Before writing about building other people up, I feel that it's important to talk about you. The leading cause for instability in otherwise thriving networks is that a leader is asking others to make a sacrifice he or she has not yet made. You can never ask more of someone else than you have given yourself. So before you try to build up others, make sure your own commitment is solid.

All this talk of commitment and sacrifice can make your business seem like a pretty serious undertaking. Well, it is. You're investing your time and effort into it, and there is a lot of potential benefit to be had. You have made a decision to build a business, and that's not something to be taken lightly. In addition to that, you're also asking other people to make a commitment. You're asking them to put their trust in you, and that's not something to be taken lightly, either.

SERVANTS AND CONTRIBUTORS

WHEN YOU INVITE SOMEONE to join your organization, you are asking them to fill one of two roles: to be either a *servant* or a *contributor*. Servants are people who render service to a group. They give of themselves to further the interests of the group, but their own interests are subordinated. In laymen's terms, we call these people 'followers.' They help achieve the success of the group without having a real stake in it.

Even in volunteer organizations, some people take on the role of servants. They make the sacrifices, but they rarely see the benefits. They are behind the scenes – often by choice. They are members of the group but not full-fledged participants. They are so heavily invested in service that they rarely see the larger picture. Often, servants are the backbone of an organization, and at the same time they are its weakest link. You see, the nature of the servant's commitment is reciprocal. In return for service, the servant expects something from the leader. These expectations take many forms, but they all fall under a single heading: the servant or follower *surrenders responsibility to the leader and expects in one way or another to be taken care of.*

In the network marketing paradigm, the servant role is obsolete. We all work for ourselves, and each of us is a full participant in the group. Unfortunately, old habits die hard. A surprising number of new entrepreneurs find themselves surrendering responsibility for their own success to someone else, in return for their service. In other words, they leave the traditional paradigm but they don't leave behind the traditional relationship. This oversight, in my view, is a leading cause of disappointment and failure. When you make a break with the old paradigm, it must be a total break, and you must seize and hold the responsibility for your own success.

That's where the second role comes into play, the role of the *contributor.* A contributor makes a commitment and a sacrifice to be a part of the group, but he or she enjoys full membership – carrying responsibilities but also receiving benefits. A contributor brings unique abilities to the table and actually shares in some leadership tasks, as well. If a servant is a follower, a contributor becomes a full partner in the enterprise.

Network marketing was designed for contributors. In the new paradigm, no one asks you to act against your own interests, or to subordinate your interests to someone else's. Instead, you actually build other people as you build yourself. By seeing to your own organization, you strengthen other groups. By benefiting from the leadership of your upline, you also provide leadership to your downline. You make a contribution to the success of the entire group, and at the same time you get a full share of the benefits that success entails.

Now the question is, what role do you play? What is the nature of your commitment right now to your business? Have you maintained responsibility for your own success? Have you made the commitment and the sacrifice to be a full-fledged member of your organization? If so, then you can invite others to do the same. If not – if you have played the role of the servant more than the contributor – it's time to take back responsibility for your success and become a full-fledged member of the team!

EDIFICATION

WE'VE TALKED ABOUT your role in the organization. Now, let's turn our attention to what you can do for other people. Building people is one of the most important things you can do in network marketing. When we say 'building people,' we're talking about a lot of different things, but let's look at just a few of the things you build through the process we call *edification*:

1. YOU BUILD CONFIDENCE

The greatest challenge facing entrepreneurs today is a lack of confidence in their personal ability. The uncertainty of the traditional paradigm has convinced more and more people to seek alternatives, and yet only a handful act. Why? Because most simply do not believe they can do it. This isn't a rational issue. It's emotional. They don't *feel* they can do it. Yes, they know in their heads they have talent. Yes, they know in their heads people just like them have done it. But they don't *feel* it inside. They have information but they lack confidence. Through edification, you can build that confidence.

2. YOU BUILD COMMITMENT

People will forsake their very lives before abandoning a deeply held commitment. Not because of the strength of their beliefs – many of us believe strongly about things without being ready to sacrifice for them – but because of their sense of ownership. They have a stake in the group, and they are not going to leave that behind. When you build other people, you elevate their standing in the group. That raises their level of commitment, their sense of ownership. Soon, you find that the people you've built up are just as committed as you are – in fact, you may find them working to build you up in the future!

3. YOU BUILD CREDIBILITY

Edification is also a tool for establishing credibility. Decisions are made in an emotional context where the primary catalyst is trust. By building up a third party in the eyes of your prospect, you can establish a level of credibility for that person that they could never manage on their own. It's as simple as adjusting the listener's attitude towards the information. I used a form of this technique in the last chapter, before discussing the relationship between the system, duplication and the culture of achievement. I told you we were about to cover very important information, the deepest things we had encountered so far in the book. Prepared like that, you were ready to look for the meaning of what I wrote. Even if I hadn't expressed it well, your attention to the information insured that you gleaned something new from it. Edification works the same way in personal relationships. You can turn an ordinary conversation into a learning experience simply by building up the speaker in the mind of a prospect before hand. It's a powerful learning technique.

4. YOU BUILD RELATIONSHIPS

Edification builds people and at the same time builds your relationships with them. It's no coincidence that the people who have the best relationships are the ones who build up others. By nature, we appreciate the people who appreciate us. When we sense genuine common ground, commitment comes easily. People who learn to edify surround themselves with a network of strong relationships, relationships where they receive as much edification as they give.

WHAT IS EDIFICATION?

THE WORD *edification* literally means to build people up. In the past, edification was a word straight out of the vocabulary of moral character. Educators used the term to indicate some activity or literature that would build character in its participants. Classic literature was said to be edifying because it gave its readers sound principles and moral precepts. Today, there is still an empowering moral dimension to edification. When you build people up you inspire in them the confidence to live up to their best impulses.

Speaking practically, edification is a habit of discovering other people's contributions and making them known. I call it a 'habit' because it is something you train yourself to do constantly, with all people, not selectively to gain a particular advantage. I call it a process of discovery, because edification requires substance – the things you say have to be true, and that means you have to discover them for yourself. Edification isn't flattery. The point isn't to make people feel good momentarily. Rather, *the goal is to let them know that their contribution is visible and appreciated.*

Edification expresses itself in both words and deeds. For convenience, we tend to discuss it in terms of what we say. In fact, some people believe that edification is wholly verbal, that it consists entirely of *saying* good things about other people. Naturally, it's more than this. Edification is an act of visible appreciation, and it expresses itself both in words and deeds. You can edify your sponsor by telling people he is a heart-felt speaker. You can edify him even more by driving two hundred miles to hear him speak! You get the idea.

Each act of edification involves three participants: the *actor*, the *object*, and the *audience*. You are the actor, the person doing the edifying. The object is the person you are expressing appreciation of – in the example above, your sponsor. The audience is the person or people who witness your message. Each party benefits in a different way. Your audience benefits by being made to share your appreciation of the object. The object benefits by being the focus of appreciation, which builds credibility and confidence. You benefit by strengthening your relationship with the object and increasing the receptiveness of your audience. Edification is a true win-win scenario.

SINCERITY

FOR EDIFICATION TO BE effective, it has to be real. You have to mean it. Insincere edification is both useless and dangerous. All the things sincere edification builds are destroyed when the appreciation is insincere. Sincerity is a necessary ingredient for effective edification.

What this means is that you have to take the process of discovery and appreciation seriously. You have to find a real reason to appreciate people, and then really appreciate them. Your edification must be an expression of what you feel, not a technique for building confidence. Edification only builds when it is ethical.

This is a bigger challenge than you may realize, because as a society, we tend to be unappreciative. We crave appreciation much more than we are willing to give it. This fundamental selfishness must be overcome before you can genuinely edify other people. Otherwise, every time you build another person up, you'll feel like you're tearing yourself down. If you're accustomed to pointing out the bad in other people, you'll need to make a major change before you can edify successfully.

Of course, it's much easier to point out other people's shortcomings. No one is perfect, and looking through ruthless eyes none of us *deserve* edification. In the traditional paradigm, we tear people down to such an extent that our contempt has become institutionalized as humor. When you look at the success of the (admittedly very funny) *Dilbert* books, you have to remember that it is built on the fact that people think their bosses are incompetent, their co-workers are fools, and their friends are less deserving than they are. Not a very pretty picture of the world when you take out the punchlines.

You may say, "OK, so I have to start finding something good to say about people?" You remember what your teachers always said: *if you don't have something good to say, don't say anything at all.* Well, it's not that easy. With the set of eyes you brought over from the traditional paradigm, you can squint at people all day without seeing something worth praising. No, before you can edify others, you have to start seeing them differently.

Go back to the Core Values. Freedom, equality, individual worth and love – these are things that other people deserve just as much as you. These are things other people are striving for just as hard as you. When you look at people, you have to stop seeing what they are and start seeing what they are striving to become. *The nobility of each individual lies in his or her aspirations.* When people begin to act on those aspirations, they deserve our respect, appreciation and as much edification as we can possibly give them.

As a rule, we judge others for what they did and judge ourselves for what we intended. It's not fair, but as long as we're judging that's how it comes out. Of course, there is an alternative, and that is to stop judging people and start edifying them.

EDIFYING YOUR UPLINE

IF YOU EVER HAVE the opportunity to talk to someone who quit building their network marketing business, you'll find that one of the first people they blame is their sponsor. If you ever have the opportunity to see a new achiever recognized on stage, you'll see that one of the first people they thank is their sponsor. The obvious conclusion would be that some people have bad sponsors and some people have good sponsors. It's the obvious conclusion, and it's wrong. The fact is, everyone has a good sponsor, and everyone has a human sponsor. In other words, no matter how hard a sponsor tries, he or she can't do everything.

The difference here isn't in the quality of the sponsor – it's a difference in the outlook of the speaker. Successful people appreciate the opportunity their sponsor has given them and unsuccessful people do not. In fact, this gratitude (or lack of it) is a factor in the success or failure of the individual, because it illustrates the person's understanding of his or her own responsibility. Successful achievers are grateful for the opportunity to create their own business. Non-achievers are disappointed that they were expected to build their own business – they expected someone else to take that responsibility. If you examine your attitude towards your own sponsor, you can get an idea of where you stand in this regard.

Let's face it, sponsors deserve all the appreciation they get. They overcame their natural inhibition and fear of rejection. They thought enough of you to share an opportunity. They took a chance in the hope that you would see the value of what they were offering. The odds are, for every person who said "Yes," several said "No." But your sponsor stuck with it and didn't give up. Your sponsor made the opportunity available to you.

In sharing the opportunity, your sponsor did not take responsibility for your success. He or she gave you an opening and may have even helped you get started. But the responsibility, obviously, is yours. Nothing your sponsor does will make you successful if you aren't building the business, and if you are building the business, there's not a whole lot more your sponsor can do but set the right example. Even if your sponsor sets an imperfect example, you have to realize we all make mistakes. By introducing you to the opportunity your sponsor made a gesture of good faith that you should always be grateful for.

The same is true of your upline. Each level of an organization is like a generation in a family tree. Your upline merits the kind of respect you would give to family ancestors. They merit this not because of anything they do but because of where they are and what they represent. After all, you don't love and respect your parents and grandparents because of any material gain you expect from them. You love and respect them for who they are, where they've been, and the opportunity they've given you. The analogy holds true in your organization. Because they were there, because they served as a conduit in offering you the opportunity, your upline deserves to be edified.

PERSONAL AND CORPORATE EDIFICATION

LET ME INTERRUPT HERE to say that there are two forms of edification: *personal* and *corporate*. You may not know your upline personally, so you aren't in a position to appreciate their personal traits and values. You can still appreciate them corporately for the role they've played in bringing you into the organization. Corporate edification can extend to include the entire organization and the leadership of the company itself. You may not know these people personally yet, but you do know what they've accomplished and the part they've played in making the opportunity available to you. In that sense, they certainly merit your appreciation.

In Nutrition For Life, you will often see this kind of corporate edification in action. I have heard people I've never met before take the stage and passionately edify my partners and I for what we've done, and I'll tell you something: it always boosts my confidence and I always make a point of getting to know that person better.

Corporate edification is important, and it goes a long way toward showing prospects and new distributors how to properly value the opportunity. But personal edification is really the heart of the matter. It's easy to look at a respected leader and find something to edify. You can simply repeat what you've heard other people say. It's important to build up the leaders, and they certainly benefit from it. But just think of the benefit to people who aren't usually edified? Personal edification is powerful because you may be the first person ever to spot some special trait or ability of a sponsor or downline distributor. You can have an untold impact on a person's life through personal edification.

ENCOURAGING YOUR DOWNLINE

EDIFICATION IS MORE than acknowledging people who have done something for you. Edification often acts as a form of encouragement. When you look at your downline distributors, you can see something they may not recognize yet: *potential*. You can transform their outlook on the business by seeing what they are capable of and appreciating it.

One of the things I learned as a coach was that my players had an inordinate amount of respect for what I said. A good word from me went a long way. If I told them they were doing something well, nothing anyone else had to say mattered. By the same token, if I pointed out a mistake, it really hit home. Sometimes, I found that I could encourage a player to develop abilities he never really practiced before just by letting him know I thought he could do it. This wasn't a new discovery for me – it's exactly what my coaches had done with me. "You could run that race two seconds faster," a coach might say to me. Maybe it was a casual remark, something he hadn't really thought about. But in my mind he was making a judgement based on years of experience: just by looking at me, he could tell I was capable of doing better. After that, I believed it, too. If I ran that race too slow, I would tell myself, "You can run this race at least two seconds faster!" And sure enough, I did. Edification can be a powerful motivator.

The moment you sponsor your first person into the business, you have an organization to nurture. For each member of your group to reach their full potential, someone has to point out what they're capable of. A new distributor has no idea what he or she can do. New distributors have no idea how many people they should show the plan to each week. They have no idea how many invitations they should make. Their own expectations are based entirely on what their sponsor tells them. Early on, a sponsor has incredible power to shape expectations – for better or worse. I've known people who have sponsored eight new distributors into the business in just a week, all because their sponsor believed they could do it. On the other hand, I know people who have done much less than they thought they could, because someone 'warned' them not to set their sights too high.

The greatest leaders in history are the ones who learned to see the potential in so-called 'ordinary' people. They developed and encouraged the people around them instead of seeking out 'extraordinary' people somewhere else. The fact is, we are *all* ordinary, but we *all* have extraordinary potential. The people who stand out as exceptionally capable are simply the ones who have begun to fulfill that potential. That's why your role as an encourager is so important. If you build them up and encourage them, you can start with ordinary people and end up with extraordinary achievers!

WHERE TO EDIFY

By now, we have a good idea of the form and content of edification. Let's look at the context – in other words, *where* to edify. The simple answer, of course, is everywhere. Edification is appropriate and effective in every business building context. You should make a habit of building up other people as a part of any other activity you engage in. When you attend a meeting or training event, you can take advantage of the opportunity to edify during conversations and breaks. When you show the plan, you can incorporate edification of the company, your upline and people in your organization. When you are asked to take on some task or responsibility by local leaders, you can use your new influence as an avenue for building people up. Every occasion offers opportunities to edify.

Even so, it's important to consider some principles to help you make the most of these opportunities:

1. PRIVATE CONVERSATIONS

The most common venue for edification is the private conversation, either in person or on the phone. Edification starts here, because if you *don't* edify in private, any public edification will seem hypocritical to people who know you. You have two distinct opportunities during every conversation. First, you can let the other person know how much you appreciate them. It doesn't have to be a flowery acknowledgement, just something practical and reassuring: "You know, I'm really pumped up now that you're involved with us!" The point is to let the other person know that you feel they're a valuable addition to the team. "I've been thinking about what you said last week . . ." is another good approach: make reference to a specific thing the person has said or done that has made an impact on you. Your second opportunity is to edify a third party, so that the person you're talking to can share your opinion – "You know, another good person to talk to about this is my sponsor, Mike. He's helped me a lot with this kind of thing." Simply direct attention to someone else you admire and respect, and explain a little bit about how this third party could benefit the person you're talking to.

2. AT MEETINGS

Everyone gets excited at meetings, and this is one of the easiest environments for edification. At the same time, it's easy to get caught up in the moment and forget to do your part. When I attend meetings, I make a mental list of the people I want to edify at some point during the event. Sometimes I recommend that one leader get in touch with another I've just spoken to. Sometimes I want to draw people's attention to an up and coming distributor. Sometimes I just want to say 'thanks' for a thoughtful gesture. For me, providing third party validation is a way to help people connect with one another. I approach it this way: "Who do I want to put this person in touch with?" In a meeting environment, edification is a form of enthusiastic referral.

3. ON STAGE

When you are invited on stage or into the spotlight in any way, you have an obligation to edify. Like an actor receiving an Oscar, you should thank the people who helped you get there. Here's a good formula: start by expressing gratitude to your sponsor. Then, single out a special person in the business who has been an inspiration to you, and share a quick lesson you've learned from this person. When you're on stage, make your statements utterly positive. This is not the time to single out the people who *didn't* help. Use your time in the spotlight to thank and encourage the people who did.

4. TELLING YOUR STORY

You will often be called upon to 'share your story,' to explain how you got involved in the business and how it has changed your life. Your story is one of the most inspirational tools you have. It has the power to stay in people's minds and be repeated. A good story creates an emotional bond between the teller and the listener – and it's the perfect opportunity to edify. When you tell your story, don't make it a 'me' story – make it a 'we' story. Include the people who have made a difference in your life. Mention the lessons they taught you along the way. Not only will this enrich your story but it will also help strengthen your bonds with the people who've helped you succeed.

BUILDING PEOPLE MAKES A DIFFERENCE

CAN YOU BUILD a business without building people? I don't think so. Building people is essential to every aspect of success – values, relationships, and responsibility. While the traditional paradigm still encourages you to surpass others to get ahead, network marketing lets you build up others to build up yourself.

Building people is a skill you can use outside the business world, too. In fact, edification breaks down the wall between your personal and professional lives. Suddenly, you are taking the values and beliefs from your personal life with you to work! What a revolutionary idea. And although these techniques were perfected for network marketing, they work in the traditional paradigm, too. Many people who have built part-time network marketing businesses have reported advancing in the traditional job market too as a result of what they've learned. Building people is the starting point for success in any business.

When we first talk about making a difference in people's lives, we usually think of things like helping the poor, taking care of the sick, or employing the jobless. In other words, we conjure up very worthy but fairly abstract ideas of what making a difference means. Usually, we're talking about making a difference in the lives of strangers – or worse, hypothetical people, people we aren't even sure exist. Edification is a way to make a difference in the lives of people you know, people you care about. It's a way of expressing your appreciation and a way of assuring people of their value and worth. When you practice edification, you make the Core Values a reality in someone's life.

That may seem far removed from the world of business, but it isn't. The challenge most businesses face isn't the lack of talented people, it's the lack of people using their talents. Most troubled companies could turn themselves around if their employees began to recognize their potential and took a stake in the business. The only reason this doesn't happen more is that we have a generation of managers who believe that things like freedom, equality, individual worth and love belong at home, in the church, or at the training seminar. They rob their business of success because they rob it of its soul.

You have an opportunity to change that. You have an understanding of the importance of the Core Values, of relationships, and of edification. You have a good idea how to build people up. Over time, with more experience, you will be able to apply this knowledge to create a different kind of business, a business that draws on a whole new paradigm of achievement. All you have to do is take the concepts you've discovered here and the techniques available through the system and apply them. In other words, all you have to do is translate these thoughts and ideas into actions.

BUILDING PEOPLE TAKES TIME

SOMETIMES YOU HEAR an inspirational story where just one kind word at the right time made all the difference. Well, that's the exception, not the rule. Human psychology is such that we do not allow ourselves to be built up too easily or too quickly. When other people compliment us or point us out to others as special, our sub-conscious finds some way to cut us back down to size. It's a useful defense mechanism that keeps us from getting a big head, but it can sometimes undermine an already fragile belief level.

Some people require months or even years of edification before they begin to reach their full potential. Others respond quickly and begin to grow right away. Don't assume that edification doesn't 'work' if you don't see immediate results. Always remember that building people takes time.

Edification occurs in the context of a relationship, and relationships do their good spread out over time. That's why I encourage you to make a habit of consistently edifying the people you believe in, regardless of what 'results' you may or may not see. No one, no matter how far they go, will ever stop needing edification. And no one, no matter how gradual their advance is, will fail to benefit from it. When you edify, do it based on your own belief, not on any effects you see. In time, edification will pay its dividend.

BUILDING BELIEF

BUILDING PEOPLE MEANS building *freedom*, building *equality*, building *worth* and building *love* – in other words, instilling the Core Values. But it also means building belief. In fact, if there is one thing edification is tailor-made to accomplish it is building a strong level of belief. Beginning when they are prospects, you can use edification to build people into motivated, committed achievers.

To begin with, edification provides third-party validation. Edification makes it 'OK' to believe in the opportunity because some respected third party gives it credence. An uncertain prospect can always fall back on the idea that it's not their credibility at stake but that third party's. "This guy is an expert, and he seems to think there's something to this," the prospect says. This is a good way to overcome initial misgivings about alternatives to the traditional paradigm – and a good way to answer skeptical co-workers!

Edification focuses new distributors on more successful mentors they can follow. This helps alleviate the pressure to succeed right away by demonstrating that there are intelligent successful people who see what you are doing and agree that it is correct. Again, the relief this can provide to an inexperienced networker is substantial. As long as the new distributor sees that the leaders are respected and knowledgeable, he or she will continue to grow in belief.

At the same time, as the business grows, the new distributors will have cause to believe in themselves. That's where edification from a sponsor or upline distributor is priceless – we've moved from third-party validation to personal validation! Until a person has actually built a downline, he or she simply doesn't know if they can do it or not. The belief they receive through edification is essential in keeping them focused until they see results of their own.

Finally, as a distributor becomes successful in his or her own right, edification from leaders helps to affirm their commitment and keep them focused on doing the right things long enough consistently. Throughout the business building process, edification provides a reserve of belief to draw on in times of doubt or challenge. When you edify and are edified in return, you become a part of the community in a way unlike any other. You know you belong, and that knowledge serves as a bulwark to keep you motivated, enthusiastic and determined to succeed.

ONE OF THE MOST POWERFUL FORCES in any person's life is the knowledge that someone else believes in them. When you build up other people, that message comes through loud and clear. Edification is one of the most profound expressions of belief in this business. When we edify one another, we tell the world we're standing together. We say that, no matter what his or her shortcomings may be, I believe they can make it – I believe they are important to this business and to my success. In a world where people have become cynical about business and even life in general, there are few messsages more inspiring than this one.

CHAPTER NINE
Making A Living

This book began with a look at a modern paradox – the decision between making a living and making a difference – and we discovered that in network marketing many people, myself included, have found a way to make a difference *and* make a living, too. In the course of eight chapters we have looked at the essential concepts of network marketing: the Core Values, residual impact, duplication, the system and more – all the tools you need to make a living in the new paradigm. We have also addressed one of the fundamental questions each of us faces at the start of a network marketing business: "Can I do it?" The answer, if you follow the principles set out in this book, is *yes*.

Success will not come overnight, and it will not be effortless. You will have to earn your achievements, just as you do in the traditional paradigm. The difference, of course, is that the new paradigm values your contribution differently. You benefit directly from the work you do, and you continue to benefit over time. You lead your own business, rather than taking orders from someone else. You magnify your own efforts by increasing the size of your organization. And all along, you avoid the substantial risk that accompanies start-up businesses in the traditional world.

You can make a living with network marketing. That's the discovery more and more people are making at the close of the twentieth century. Networking is a practical, efficient way to supplement – and even replace – your regular income. It is a great way to start your own business and get a taste of freedom. If you build it properly, network marketing will meet all your expectations and then some.

SUPPLEMENTAL INCOME

MANY OF THE PEOPLE coming to network marketing today have no intention of leaving their regular job. Some are professionals who trained for years to qualify for their positions. Others are people doing a job they love that simply doesn't pay enough. Most feel they would appreciate their jobs more and do better at them if they just had a reliable supplemental income. For them, network marketing is an ideal part-time home-based business.

For years, people have been saying that this industry creates more millionaires than any other. I've never seen a statistic on this – it's always second- or third-hand information – but whether it's true or not doesn't really matter. Becoming a millionaire is a nice dream, but it's so abstract that it hardly motivates a person living in the 'real' world. Most people aren't so much interested in becoming millionaires as they are in paying all the monthly bills and still having money left over, still having something for savings. A far-away abstraction simply cannot motivate people like a reliable, realistic supplemental income does.

Network marketing doesn't promise to make you a millionaire. It doesn't promise to transform you into a jet-set celebrity moving back and forth between high-priced watering holes. Instead, this business offers a practical avenue for people who want to earn a better living. Yes, your network marketing business can provide *much more* than that, but let's focus for just a moment not on best case scenarios but on your day-to-day dreams.

If you make a serious part-time commitment to building your business, it should take between two and five years to build a sizeable residual income. During this time you will be engaged in three basic activities: *moving product, increasing the size of your organization*, and *participating in your organization's culture*. The goal of every business is to move product. In network marketing, all commissions are based on product transactions by you and your organization. It stands to reason that the larger the organization, the more product sales volume – and therefore, the more income – you will generate. Your participation in training, meetings and other activities insures that you maintain your focus and effectiveness over time. These three components, duplicated part-time by you and your growing organization over a two-to-five year period, generally result in sustained supplemental – and even replacement – income.

It sounds easy, and on paper it is. The unpredictable factor, the variable, is your commitment level. Two things can happen that will interfere with your success: 1) *you can quit*, or 2) *you can lose focus and stop building*. They are both catastrophes and they are both the direct result of your commitment being tested over time and found lacking. Two to five years isn't a long time – not compared to the twenty or more years it takes in the traditional world – but people are notorious short-term thinkers. We are all pre-disposed to take less than our fair share rather than wait. We are prepared to do the right things, but not always *long enough*, and not always *consistently*. So what can we do about it?

First, *we can have realistic expectations*. Unless you are a rare achiever, you will not become a millionaire by building your business part-time. You will not become a millionaire within several months or even a couple of years of starting a part-time business. Let's be realistic. Whatever your long-term goal is, you need to have attainable, well-founded short-term objectives. One of the most tragic things I have seen in my lifetime is a person who throws away a thriving part-time business, with lots of potential, because it didn't generate 'millions' soon enough. What a waste! Your business, even worked part-time, has so much potential – *but it can only be realized over time!*

Second, *we can eliminate the exit strategies.* When you present a business plan for a traditional start-up, one of the common features you include is an 'exit strategy.' This strategy isn't always as gloomy as it sounds – some exit strategies involve getting the company to the point where it can go public or be bought out by a larger company. On other hand, investors want to know what you plan on doing if things don't work out. In other words, how are you going to make a graceful exit when and if the time comes? When Tom Schreiter, Jana Mitcham and I founded Nutrition For Life, I guess we didn't know enough about making business plans, because we never plotted an exit strategy. There was never any question of quitting. Now, there were times in the company's history where outsiders felt we had gone as far as we could. There were times when we were advised to move on. We didn't listen. We simply hadn't made an accommodation for failure. Nutrition For Life is now a thriving multi-million dollar international corporation. Based on my experience, I suggest dispensing with the exit strategies. When you're working with a proven system, you don't need criteria for failure, you need a commitment to succeed.

Third, *we can take ownership.* One reason some people give up on their business is that they never really took possession of it. As a rule, we don't abandon what is ours. We stick by it and make it grow at any cost. Once you've invested your time and energy into the business, anything less than success is unthinkable. When you start a Nutrition For Life business, for example, that business belongs to you. As an independent distributor, you own the business you build. You – and only you – are responsible for it. You – and only you – can make it succeed.

INCREASING YOUR COMMITMENT

BEGIN YOUR BUSINESS as a part time enterprise, but don't be surprised when, over time, it starts to merit more and more of your attention.

Many people who expected a supplemental income have built a replacement income instead. Many people who started a part-time business have increased their commitment and made it a full-time enterprise. There's certainly no obligation to do this, but if you do, it is one of the most rewarding phases in the growth of your business.

By increasing the amount of time you commit to your business, you increase your ability to build your organization. We've already seen how a larger organization leads to more income. Instead of showing the plan to one or two people in your spare time, you can devote a larger portion of time to introducing more people to the business. You can also spend more time working with new distributors and helping them duplicate the system.

As a rule, I do not recommend that you begin your business working full-time, although that is a worthy goal. Your business will tell you when it is time to increase your commitment. Even if you keep your traditional job and build only a supplemental income, there are times when you will want to put more effort into the business just to give it some added momentum. Above all, the business is flexible. You have the freedom to increase your time commitment and still take time off when you need to.

I like to compare building a network marketing business to building a fire. Today, most houses have gas fireplaces, which spoils the analogy, so I want you to imagine an old-fashioned wood-burning fireplace. The first time I lit a fire like this, I was surprised how much work it took. I had to find kindling, and then I had to get it to light. That was just the beginning, because getting the wood to burn wasn't always easy. If I used newspaper for kindling, the paper sometimes burnt to a crisp before any of the wood caught fire. In the early stages, I had to pay attention to the details. Then, when the fire was lit, I had to feed it. Feeding a fire produces a lot of light and a lot of heat. When the crackling subsides, the flame maintains itself with just a little intervention – you reach a plateau where you can relax for a while.

You can build the fire as big as you want. You may want a raging blaze, or you may want a modest flame. It all depends on what you put into it. You can start off small and build it up over time. But if you neglect it, the fire will eventually burn out. Even when it's burning bright and confident, the fire must be tended.

Your business requires some effort to get started right. Even once it's up and running, your business will never take care of itself. At times it will burn bright and require very little from you to keep going. At other times it will need to be fed or it will burn out. As long as you are tending it, you can decide what you want it to do and feed it accordingly. Over time you can increase your commitment and your business will produce more. You may not be ready to do that yet, in which case you can keep the fire burning until you are. In my experience, most people who make the two to five year commitment end up making an even greater commitment when they see the results – building the business can really get you fired up.

A BETTER LIFE

YOU CAN MAKE A LIVING in the new paradigm, but that's not why people choose network marketing. Instead, they choose networking because they want to make more than a living. In many cases, they already make ends meet – they may even be well off. They choose network marketing because it offers the opportunity not just for a living but for *a better life.*

In the traditional paradigm, it often seems that nice guys finish last. Holding on to your principles is considered to be the ultimate naivete, a recipe for disaster in the real world. You can make a lot of money in the traditional business world and never enjoy it. You can't help but think of the people who had to suffer so you could succeed. You step on someone else's fingers every time to take another rung on the corporate ladder. You can make a living, but you can't always live with yourself.

Even if you hold on to your principles, there is a price to pay for success in the traditional paradigm. Consider some of the challenges even successful people face:

1. SUCCESSFUL EXECUTIVES WORK HARDER THAN EVER

The nine-to-five job doesn't end at five anymore, and it doesn't take breaks on the weekend, either. As corporations downsize and stay leaner the people who are left have to pick up the slack, working harder than ever. To stay on top in the traditional paradigm, you have to make a substantial commitment of time, sometimes sacrificing the things that matter most. You also have to contend with the rising tide of stress, a by-product of the uncertainty that's running rampant in the nine-to-five world. Job security – even for top performers – is a thing of the past.

2. COMPETITION IS FIERCE

If you have a good job, you can be sure there are a number of qualified candidates out there who would like to take it from you. Despite attempts by business gurus to promote cooperation, competition is fiercer today than ever. The pressure to perform at the highest levels is compounded by the knowledge that if you let up, even for a short period, your job is in jeopardy.

3. NO TIME FOR FAMILY

The single-minded focus required to stay on top of the workload and survive in the competitive world pushes your family out of the picture. You miss birthdays and special occasions. You work late time and time again. You don't see your family anymore. In their eyes, you've made a choice: the job is more important. No amount of explaining can make up for not being there. Travel demands are another problem. When young job candidates list "willing to travel" as one of their strong points, they don't know what they're asking for. The corporate world is becoming increasingly mobile and far-flung. Top executives work out of their briefcases, conducting business over the cellular phone during the break between flights. The disruption this brings to your family is enormous. Of course, your relationships with extended family and friends suffer, too. Instead of seeing you, they only hear about you second-hand. Meanwhile, you tell yourself there is light at the end of the tunnel, but the fact is, the work isn't going to go away. Unless you shift paradigms, the dynamics will stay the same and the problems will only get worse.

THESE ARE ALL FAMILIAR CHALLENGES in the traditional paradigm. In fact, much of the innovation in business thinking over the past decade has been aimed at addressing these concerns. Unfortunately, technology and the global market have far out-paced our ability to cope effectively with the alienation and disconnectedness that results. These are issues that are getting worse, not better.

In comparison, the demands placed on your time and energy by a new network marketing business are minimal. The major advantage, of course, is that you're in charge of the schedule. You can decide where your time is best spent. Here are some other factors to keep in mind:

1. INCREASED FREEDOM, NOT INCREASED WORKLOAD

Over time, a successful network marketing business generates residual income. That means, as time goes on, the benefits you derive from your actions multiply. Instead of seeing your workload double, you can see your residual gains increase. In the traditional paradigm, hard work leads to advancement, which leads to harder work. In network marketing, hard work leads to residual impact, and that leads to increased freedom. You are always responsible for you own success – but that's *all* you're responsible for!

2. COOPERATION, NOT COMPETITION

In network marketing, you work *with,* not against, other distributors. Your position is always secure. When people in your organization are successful, rather than detracting from your achievements, your benefits are enhanced. When you build your own business, distributors in your upline and downline benefit from the activity. In the mid-1980s, many people were calling network marketing 'cooperative' marketing because instead of putting members of the sales force at odds with one another, this marketing concept brought them together. Today, the cooperative aspect of network marketing is very attractive to people who are tired of the rat race.

3. TIME FREEDOM

Rather than monopolizing your time, your commitment to network marketing actually frees you to make other commitments. Of all the freedoms you can earn through building a business, none is more precious than time freedom. Your quality of life is determined just as much by how you spend your time as how much money you make. Time freedom adds value to your income by bringing more enjoyment to your life. It gives you the opportunity to fully participate once again in your family's life. It gives you the chance to invest your effort into other worthy causes. It gives you a license to 'be there' when important things are happening in your life, instead of hearing about them over the phone while you put in more overtime. Time freedom is truly liberating.

AT TIMES, life is about making hard choices, but there are some choices you shouldn't have to make. Network marketing gives you the opportunity to earn financial and time freedom, to structure your commitments in accord with your own priorities. We all have to make sacrifices, but with network marketing you won't have to sacrifice the things that really matter. You can enjoy success, keep your principles, and still have time for your family. No wonder successful distributors are so grateful to their sponsors for sharing the opportunity with them!

CHAPTER TEN

Making A Difference

WE LEARN BY EXAMPLE, but it isn't enough to have a good example set before us. To profit from the experience we have to be receptive and actively seeking improvement. Wisdom only benefits those who are pre-disposed to become wise. In fact, with the right mindset, you can convert even imperfect information into valuable knowledge – as I hope you will do with this book. Here, in the final chapter, I am aware of all the important things that time and space constraints have forced me to omit. My goal for this book, however, is not to complete your network marketing education but rather to begin it (or, in some cases, to begin it anew). In my journey, I have had the opportunity to learn from many great mentors, and it is their knowledge, not mine, which I have presented here. Now, in time, with what you know and can still learn by re-reading this book, you can take this information and go farther with it than any of us have. You have the opportunity to surpass the achievements of those who have gone before you – by building *on* them.

Traditionally, success in business and success in life have been at odds with one another. To get ahead, people have been expected to sacrifice the people and things they actually are working *for*. To put food on the table, they don't get home from work until the family has already eaten. In the ivory towers of education, there has always been a suspicion of those who want to achieve success. Wealth and wrong have been grouped together in the popular imagination. So it is interesting when you find an example that goes against all this. In his book *Money and the Meaning of Life*, philosopher Jacob Needleman describes a discussion where a successful businessman has been added to a panel of professors to discuss the role of money in society. Of course, the thrust of the argument is that money and the desire for it have played a negative role in our world, best exemplified by the stereotype of the 'evil' corporation and the uncaring millionaire. In opposition to this rhetoric, the businessman puts forward a modest, personal objection: yes, the inordinate love of money is wrong, but in life, having money does seem to *help*. Success often frees an individual to make a positive difference in the world. Indeed, as Cephalus explains to Socrates in the *Republic*, wealth helps a good man fulfill his obligations and keep a clear conscience.

One of the reasons why making a difference and making a living seem to exist at opposite poles is the erroneous notion, so popular in today's cynical culture, that *to achieve success you must somehow compromise your integrity.* If anything, this book was written to refute this hollow claim and to demonstrate that – to achieve true and lasting success – you must *never* compromise on what you hold dear. Again drawing on Plato's *Republic*: "No wealth can ever make a bad man at peace with himself." Not only do nice guys *not* finish last, but 'nice' guys are also the only ones who finish at all!

KEEPING UP APPEARANCES

EVEN THE CYNICS acknowledge that values and ethical behavior are a cornerstone of success. In his infamous book *The Prince*, Machiavelli said that it is better for a leader to be feared than to be loved. He went on to specify a number of ruthless, amoral tactics a leader could use to grab and hold political power. Interestingly enough, one of these techniques is to 'seem' to be ethical, pious, and worthy of respect. In essence, the leader should appear to be governed by values and principles, but in reality operate pragmatically. As we can see from today's political landscape, Machiavelli's advice has been influential in the extreme!

But why should a person who wields all the power worry about what his followers think of him? If they see him for what he is, so what? Why did the leading advocate of ruthless political pragmatism feel the need to cloak his activities in a veil of trustworthiness? There are many explanations, but I believe one of the most persuasive is the fact that no matter how 'effective' ruthless leadership may seem, principled leadership is what inspires and motivates people. Ethical leadership, grounded in respect for the follower, is what builds people's trust and devotion. If an unethical leader cannot *appear* to be ethical, he will not be the leader for long. What an irony!

Today, there are still two schools of effective action. Ruthless pragmatism is still the dominant philosophy in the traditional business paradigm. In my opinion, the prevalence of this philosophy explains the current turmoil and backlash against the modern corporate world. The second school, the school of ethical effectiveness, is the one I advocate. I maintain that it is better to be ethical than to appear to be ethical, because sooner or later the veneer of the pragmatist will rub off. On the other hand, the leader who is willing at times to act against self-interest to do what is right will always command the respect and admiration of his or her followers.

For these ethical achievers, success at making a living opens up the door to making a difference.

PEOPLE, NOT PROBLEMS

THE SMALLEST THINGS can make a difference. The mistake many people make is in supposing they cannot do enough. In the face of daunting situations, they revert to inaction, believing there is nothing they can really do to help. After all, some situations cannot be 'fixed.' There are times when, no matter what you do, it isn't enough to set things right.

Making a difference doesn't mean making problems go away. It doesn't mean 'fixing' other people's lives. Just because you can't do *everything* doesn't mean you can't do *something*. At its simplest, making a difference is simply *doing something* valuable.

Here is one piece of advice that can change your whole outlook on making a difference. This is the kind of thing you should copy on to an index card and carry with you, as a reminder. It is a formula I have learned over the years that has certainly made all the difference for me: *Your role is not to solve* problems *but to help* people. You cannot solve other people's problems. You cannot assume responsibility for their lives. But you can help. You can make a contribution. You can make a difference.

By nature, men like to solve problems. We are notorious for interrupting our wives as they share a dilemma to offer our quick-and-easy 'solutions.' We jump right in and say, "This is what you should have done," before we've even heard what the problem was! We listen to just enough of the situation to select the appropriate answer, whether it works for her or not.

The 'problem-solving' mentality pushes people right out of the equation. It also closes the door on the common need people have for emotional support. Instead of 'being there,' the problem-solver offers a ready-made solution. Instead of offering comfort, the problem-solver says, "If you had done what I told you, this wouldn't be happening." Problem-solvers make a difference, but not always for the better.

As a rule, the only problems you can really solve are your own. What you have to offer the rest of the world is your compassion. If you can look past the problem and see a way to help the person, you are on the way to making a positive difference. You don't have to jump in and fix everything. You just have to give a little encouragement. You just have to open a door.

Through Nutrition For Life, my partners and I have made a difference in many people's lives. That doesn't mean we've 'fixed' them. Instead, what we've done is open a door. We have made an opportunity available, and we have placed it on a firm footing. We have made it possible for people to achieve better health and financial freedom. At the same time, we haven't *given* the freedom to anyone. All we've provided is the opportunity for individuals to earn it. We can't solve other people's problems, but we can provide an opportunity for people to solve problems themselves.

In your life, the same holds true. No matter how successful you are – no matter how much you achieve – you cannot offer others more than an opportunity. But the opportunity you offer is something powerful. It can help a person regain personal responsibility and self-respect. It can help a person achieve freedom. It can help a person solve his or her own problems and go on to help other people. It can help create a legacy that can be passed on to generations to come.

Parents want to take care of the kids. We want to pave the way for them, clear all the obstacles. If we could, we would give our children everything they will ever need to face every challenge in life. If we could, we would face those challenges for them. But we come to learn that ultimately, our children have to live their own lives. The most we can offer them is opportunity. We can open doors for them, and we can raise them in such a way that they know how to walk though them. We cannot solve all their problems, but we can certainly help them along.

When you come to grips with this reality, you begin to understand what making a difference is all about. You can make a difference in the lives of everyone you meet. You can have a positive impact on the world around you. You can leave things better than how you found them. Not by writing a big check or intervening in other people's problems, but by providing opportunity.

Given the chance, people will make their way in life. The problem is, many people never do get the chance. The opportunities are technically available – the doors are open – but people just don't know how to walk through. They don't know how to take an opportunity and use it to achieve their dreams. If you will show them how, you *will* make a difference. You can give a man a fish and feed him for a day. You can teach him how to fish and feed him for a lifetime. Or, you can give him some fishing rods, and help him share the knowledge and feed his community. Making a difference means taking the opportunity you have been given, introducing it to others, and helping them share it.

LEAVING A LEGACY

MANY NETWORK MARKETING distributors share the sense that they are building something larger than themselves. They are building more than a business – they are building a legacy. They want to make a difference in the bigger arena of life. They want their actions to count towards some greater purpose, to be remembered as significant.

Let me share a story of a man who left a legacy that will not soon be forgotten. You won't find any statues erected to him. You won't find any buildings named after him or any scholarship programs bearing his name. But Carl Gleckman left a legacy that continues to be an inspiration to the men and women of Nutrition For Life to this day.

Carl brought an enthusiasm and a commitment to his network marketing business that singled him out from the beginning. He was one of the most positive people I had ever come in contact with. I meet a lot of people in my travels, at meetings and rallies around the world, and few of them leave as indelible an impression as Carl Gleckman did. He was the kind of person you couldn't get out of your mind.

I had been introduced to Carl and continued to notice him at meetings during his first months in the business. He was building an impressive organization, and doing it quickly. I had Carl pegged as the classic go-getter. I figured he brought this kind of energy to everything he did.

Because Carl Gleckman displayed the kind of enthusiasm that gets people talking, I found myself mentioning him to another distributor, someone in his organization.

"Carl sure doesn't waste any time," I said. "He's just never seems to stop."

"Well," she said. "He doesn't have any time to waste."

"What do you mean?"

"Didn't you know? Carl has been diagnosed with a terminal illness. The doctors say he hasn't got long to live."

I was stunned. "And he's building a business?"

After that, I made it a point to speak to Carl Gleckman personally. I wanted to know what was driving him. Most people in his circumstances don't exhibit this kind of enthusiasm, and they certainly don't spend their time building a business!

"I'm building more than a business," Carl said. "I'm building a legacy."

Carl explained it all to me and I was speechless. Diagnosed with a terminal illness, with only a matter of months to live, Carl Gleckman had started his Nutrition For Life business with one goal in mind: to build a legacy for his wife Millie. You see, Carl was concerned about her. He had always been the one to provide for her, and when his health was good, that was fine. But when the doctor diagnosed his condition, Carl realized that when he was gone, his paycheck would be gone, too.

"I'm building this business for Millie," Carl said, "because when I'm gone, this will be all she has. And I'm relying on *you*," he said, "to make sure that when I'm gone, this business is here for her."

For years, I had talked about how Nutrition For Life was here to stay. My partners and I had seen what happened when a company closed its doors, and we made a promise to ourselves that this would never happen with Nutrition For Life. We meant it. Even so, I never took that commitment more seriously than I did when I promised Carl Gleckman that if he built the business, it would be there for Millie when he was gone.

Now that I knew the story, I could appreciate Carl's commitment all the more. He was building the business like there was no tomorrow, because for him there wouldn't be. He worked incessantly, showing the plan, building his organization, making all kinds of audio tapes to help Millie with the business once he was gone. Knowing what I knew, I sincerely admired Carl and what he was doing.

It takes time to build the business, of course, and there are few people who could manage what Carl accomplished in such a short period of time. To make a long story short, he succeeded admirably. He created a strong, stable organization that began to create residual income. And then, regrettably, Carl passed away.

But he was not forgotten. Each month, Nutrition For Life sends a check to his wife, to Millie Gleckman, a token of the legacy Carl has left for her. To this very day, years later, Millie Gleckman still receives a commission check from Nutrition For Life. Her husband's dream is a reality, and Nutrition For Life is the protector of that dream.

Not long ago, I saw Millie Gleckman at a meeting. We had a nice conversation. She appreciated the fact that this company had remembered what Carl had done. She shared with me one of the audiotapes Carl made for her. On the plane flying home, I held that cassette in my hand. I couldn't wait to listen to it. I put it into the tape player in the car as I drove home from the airport, and for the first time in a long time, I heard the voice of Carl Gleckman sharing the plan. And I couldn't help thinking that, of all people, Carl Gleckman has made a difference.

When I shared Carl Gleckman's story at Nutrition For Life's 1997 Annual Convention, I used it to illustrate the point that distributors could rely on our company to stay the distance. I wanted to show that we took our commitment seriously, and that legacies really can be built. Today, I wonder how many people just like Carl are building the business right now. Maybe they haven't been diagnosed with a terminal illness, but something has happened in their lives that told them the time to wait was over. I opened this book sharing my own awakening experience, something as simple as a mentor showing me a glimpse of his paycheck and asking if it was enough. I have heard many other stories over the years of how some event – catastrophic in some cases, minor in others – suddenly put everything in focus.

At moments like this, the thing you think about isn't just making more money. It isn't living a more comfortable life, or having more *things*. At these moments of revelation, your thoughts are fixed on something altogether higher. To really understand what it means to make a difference, you have to hold on to that insight, that higher vision, that knowledge of something larger than yourself. You have to hold on to that legacy, the legacy you can build when you build a business.

Carl Gleckman left a legacy when all the odds were against him. He started his business with a time limit and every reason in the world not to take action. If Carl had given up, no one would have blamed him. If he had spent his final days in comfort, no one would have begrudged him that. Instead, he did something remarkable. He focused not on himself but on the people he loved, and he built a legacy that even today is a monument to what he accomplished. When I think of all the people who turn their back on opportunity, who think they can't do it, that it's too difficult or beyond reach, I just think of Carl Gleckman. What he lacked in advantages he made up in belief, and if Carl could build a legacy under circumstances like those, who are we to say 'no' when opportunity presents itself?

Have you given much thought to the legacy you will leave your family and friends, the people you love? On a national level, it seems that the greatest legacy we in the United States will leave to the next generation is a legacy of debt. I'm afraid that many of us will do the same on the personal level, too. Yes, we will leave a legacy, but not one we'd like to be remembered for. The tragedy is that every one of us has it within our power to leave a positive legacy, to make a positive difference in the world around us. It's simply a matter of commitment. If we would emulate the resolve of a man like Carl Gleckman, we could duplicate his results.

On television recently, a financial advisor was promoting his new book. He singled out members of the audience who had lost their jobs and were now in financial straits, then he showed them strategies for bringing in more income and reducing their debt. Two young ladies in particular struck me as representative. Both were single mothers with reduced incomes and mounting debt. They were both trying to raise their kids and provide opportunities for them. They were trying to get back on track. The financial advisor took a look at their cases and had to reluctantly recommend filing for bankruptcy. He really couldn't see another option. One mother started asking questions about how to file. The other just smiled. When questioned, she explained she had no intention of filing for bankruptcy, no intention of quitting. She was determined to find a way to pay off her debts and provide for her own future and the future of her family. She would find ways to increase her income, but she would not consider defaulting on her obligations. I was impressed.

That's the kind of integrity that makes all the difference. We all feel the occasional burden of our responsibilities, and the reality is, in our society, our obligations are sometimes easy to dodge. I'm not passing judgement on people who file bankruptcy – it's a legitimate option – but I want to illustrate the value of what taking the higher ground can be. Many people come to network marketing with debt, and they build a business with the express purpose of paying off that debt, fulfilling their obligations. Many people come to network marketing unable to pay the bills, unable to support their families. They build a business because they want to get on top of their situation and start calling the shots again. Other people are getting by, but they just aren't able to provide the best for their family. They build a business so they can add a little quality to the lives of the people they love. All of these people are making a difference. They are all building a business to provide a legacy.

You have the same opportunity. Armed with the knowledge in this book, you can make a living and make a difference in people's lives. You can overcome your circumstances and put yourself in charge. You can build a business by sharing an opportunity with other people. You can give them a way to change their lives, and change your own life in the process. You have a remarkable tool in your hands. Now, use it.

THE NUTRITION FOR LIFE DIFFERENCE

THROUGHOUT THIS BOOK, I've made reference to Nutrition For Life, the company founded in 1984 by myself, Jana Mitcham and Tom 'Big Al' Schreiter. I'd like to tell you a little bit about the opportunity this company provides and the way it protects the legacies of those who join us.

Jana is my sister-in-law. I married her sister Judy in 1963. Since the early 1980s, Jana and I have shared the dream of a unique network marketing company combining life-changing products and an innovative opportunity. The culmination of this dream is Nutrition For Life. The company began as a family affair, and although it has grown, it remains one today. My wife Judy helps keep things running smoothly at World Headquarters and Jana's husband

Tom heads up our new product development. Our children have gone on to play a role in the company, so you could say that Nutrition For Life is our legacy in more ways than one. Internally, the company reflects the same values that shape our business philosophy. I look at Nutrition For Life as the greatest learning experience in my life – it has given me the opportunity to work with a remarkable group of people.

Tom Schreiter is the author of the popular 'Big Al' series of network marketing handbooks and a frequent contributor to industry publications. Tom is the company's founding distributor, and his insights have helped make Nutrition For Life the distributor-conscious organization it is today. On a personal level, Tom's friendship and his sense of humor have been a comfort in many trying times. No one avoids the spotlight more than Tom Schreiter, and no one deserves more than Tom to be in it.

Together, we created something that has grown much larger than ourselves. Nutrition For Life is now a multi-million dollar international corporation with plans for expansion world-wide. We believe we have something unique to offer in this industry, something that is best summed up in the title "protectors of the dream."

A network marketing company plays many roles in the life of its distributors, but the most important is keeping the dream a distributor has built safe and secure. Doing that job well insures that Carl Gleckman and thousands more like him can trust that their legacy will endure. In the uncertain world we live in, that's quite a reassurance.

I believe very strongly in the network marketing concept, and the emergence of more and more companies over the years has been a welcome development. Today, network marketing is a fast-growing marketing segment with new opportunities emerging every day. People looking for an opportunity now have a wide number of options to choose from. We appreciate the fact that, since 1984, many thousands of achievers have made the decision to join Nutrition For Life. We aren't the only company out there, but we have worked hard to be the only company of our kind.

Our success and longevity are due to one factor alone: the remarkable character of our distributors. They are determined and talented, and they make a difference in more lives than anyone can count. They have been a source of support and inspiration for me over the years and have always made me proud to be a part of this life-changing opportunity.

TAKE AIM AND FIRE

HISTORIANS HAVE SPECULATED that, in the high-stress environment of a Civil War battle, only a portion of the soldiers actually fired their rifles. Reports have come down to us of rifles recovered after a battle that had been loaded twice, three times, or as many as ten times and never fired. In the heat of the moment, with all the complicated drills and procedures that had to be remembered, the most important part of the process was – remarkably – forgotten.

At the end of a book like this, the risk is the same. You've been primed and loaded. You've been given valuable information. You've gotten a glimpse of just how valuable an opportunity can be. You've seen that financial and time freedom are a practical, achievable reality. You're ready. Now aim and fire!

The most common reaction to new information is to want to know more. Although the desire for more knowledge is good, there is also a time for action. Once your rifle is loaded, it's time to fire. Many people today are over-loaded. They had good information and instead of taking action, they hunted down more information. Soon, they became 'experts' – they knew much more than anyone who was actually *doing* it – and by that time the rifle had been loaded so many times it was useless.

You do not need more information. You do not need further training. You do not need advanced techniques. You are loaded. You are primed and ready to fire. The target is in front of you. If you look up and down the line, you'll see that most people are loading instead of firing. But there are a few who are taking aim and pulling that trigger. Those are the people to model yourself on. They are the ones to follow.

If you had started building your business in earnest two weeks ago, you would be a different person today. Fortunately, the opportunity is still there. You can make a living in network marketing, and more importantly, you can make a difference. Or, you can just talk about it. You've been reading about it, and now the time for reading is over. The only difference between where you are right now and the people who have built long-term stable businesses is a sequence of duplicated actions. Like a drill, it requires consistency and a steady hand. You can give it both.

If you take anything away with you from this book, let it be this: *embrace the new paradigm, act according to the Core Values, and start building up people.* When you do these things long enough, consistently, you'll find yourself making a difference while you're making a living.